BIRDWATCHER'S DIARY

ROGER LOVEGROVE & PETER BARRETT
BIRDWATCHER'S DIARY

HUTCHINSON
London Melbourne Sydney Auckland Johannesburg

CONTENTS

Preface, 6

SPRING, 8

SUMMER, 52

AUTUMN, 88

WINTER, 120

Opposite: grey wagtails, dipper and magpie.

PREFACE

My interest in wildlife, and birds in particular, began at a very early age—earlier than I can remember—and although there is no doubt that being brought up in the countryside probably encouraged this interest, I fancy it would have occurred wherever I had been born. My memories of boyhood are of an endless succession of excursions and forays in several parts of England through the woods, fields and hills around home. From the fields of Oxfordshire, the beech woods of the Chilterns, the rough commons and hopfields of Herefordshire to the hills, rivers and great estuary marshes of Cumberland, day after day of wandering and exploring the open countryside engendered within me a lifelong devotion to wildlife. For twelve years now I have worked professionally in conservation and would like to think that something is now being returned in exchange for the infinite pleasure I have derived in the past.

In its way I hope that this book mirrors to some degree the pleasure and excitement which birds, with their constant ability to delight and surprise, have brought to me over the years. Season by season, I have tried to identify and recreate in these pages some of the experiences of one year. Each year has its highlights, but the events I describe, with one or two special exceptions arising from my work with the RSPB, are parallel to those that anyone who uses

their eyes and ears may experience for themselves throughout the course of twelve months.

Apart from recounting some of my own experiences *Birdwatcher's Diary* aims to help and encourage readers who, perhaps for the first time, are seeking a little more from their interest in birds than the simple pleasure of seeing them. There is a world of difference between seeing birds and watching them. To see a bird may be to admire its form, its colour, grace, and power. To *watch* the same bird is to begin to understand why its form is as it is, why its colours have evolved as they have and how the bird uses them; it is to comprehend the reason for its power and grace, and to recognize the significance, the seasonality and the individuality of its song. In these respects this book of course lays no claim to comprehensiveness; it seeks merely to open the door to the complex and fascinating lives of the everyday birds around us. At the same time it touches on a few other subjects which may serve to make birdwatching easier and more rewarding, or which demonstrate ways in which we can provide for birds and, in return, encourage their presence around our homes and gardens. Not least, the book also gives expression to Peter Barrett's superb illustrations, which, with their vivid images, textures and colour, interpret so much that no words could convey. Peter Barrett, too, is a countryman, whose gifts of observation and execution

combine to produce artwork of quite extraordinary beauty.

If there is a theme that emerges in the course of this account, it is that whereas we, as humans, may for convenience choose to break up the year into calendar units and thereby relate certain activites to particular seasons, birds tend not to fit into this convenient pattern. They display enormous variation from one species to another, nesting, migrating or flocking at times which we often find odd. Within a single species too there may be great flexibility: wood pigeons, for example, can be found nesting in almost any month of the year. So part of our understanding of birds must take into account that they have their own timetables which often do not conform to ours.

The diary itself contains, not surprisingly, a number of references to the area around my home, so perhaps a note of explanation at this point would be useful. The house where I live with my wife and family was built, many years ago, as a shooting lodge. It sits at the foot of steep hills – long since denuded of their moorland vegetation and hence of their shooting value too – a mile or so from the River Severn, where it sweeps down through the Welsh hills on its way to the English border. A small stream flows out of the hills past our house, cutting a valley so narrow and winding that there is barely room enough on the floor of it for the stream, the cul-de-sac lane and the chain of tiny meadows tucked singly into each alternating curve of the stream. The sides of the valley are steep and clad mainly in woods of oak and ash, above which lie sheep pastures running far up on to the hills; the valley is so steep-sided that even in summer the sun does not strike the house until well into the morning and has disappeared by early evening.

It is a quiet valley that, like another thousand similar Welsh valleys, pulses with wildlife throughout the year. Buzzards and ravens are daily overhead, grey wagtails and dippers on the stream; the woods are populated, in the course of a year, by over fifty species of bird. Today, as I write, it is a bright, warm mid-April day: the first pied flycatcher has arrived and is already prospecting nest-boxes, jackdaws are carrying sticks into their chimney nests and a willow warbler has sung all day long from the bank opposite. Ideal as these surroundings may seem, their richness, in terms of birdlife, is by no means unique. Most areas of Britain can prove just as rewarding for the observant birdwatcher: town parks, suburban gardens, railway lines, even city streets and motorways – the birds are there to be seen and enjoyed by everyone with a will to look for them, all the year round.

Roger Lovegrove.

SPRING

Spring

In our north-temperate latitudes spring, with its attendant sensations of energy and excitement is the great reawakening, the time of rebirth and new life. It comes not with the finality of a tropical rain season or the inevitability of an Arctic winter but in stages – with false starts, half-promises, disappointments and relapses. Climatologically, at least, it can manifest itself through warmth and sunshine at any time between early March and the end of April. We recognize it in the lengthening of the days and the emergence of new growth. Birds, physiologically sensitive to their own time clocks, will respond to the increasing hours of daylight too, but their spring – or rather the activities of theirs which *we* associate with spring – will be spread over a much longer period, from species to species, overlapping generously with winter on one side and summer on the other. Some of the summer migrants are very early arrivals.

Wheatears are bright and conspicuous early-season migrants, providing a perfect excuse to go up into the hills at a time of year when one might not otherwise do so.

The boldly marked grey, black and white males are the first visitors to arrive in spring, occasionally as early as February on the south coast or the tops of the Sussex downs, but usually not before March, after which their numbers build up towards a peak by the end of the month or in the first weeks of April. The males, migrating separately, make their first landfall a week or two before the more modestly coloured females and they come from their African wintering areas to nest in the uplands of north and west Britain, where short, sheep-grazed turf provides them with the abundant insect feeding they require to rear their successive broods.

Each spring the Young Ornithologists' Club (the junior wing of the Royal Society for the Protection of Birds, or RSPB) runs a 'phone-in' between mid-March and mid-May through which both YOC members and members of the public at large are encouraged to report the dates of their first sightings of the spring and summer migrants. In this way progressive maps are built up nationwide each year showing the arrival of our summer visitors in different parts of the country. The wheatear, being the earliest and most conspicuous of arrivals, is one of the species best covered each year.

There are one or two places I know of where I can usually rely on seeing the first cock wheatear at this time of year, often simply by driving along the mountain roads slowly and finding one flitting alongside the road or darting across the front of the car. They have favoured spots, as do many migrant species, and the little roadside quarries, or one or two particular scree slopes, are usually likely places for a sighting. I tried these first one Sunday morning but was disappointed – only five ravens spilling over the top of a rocky hill and flying noisily down the valley – so I went over the next hill and searched along the road around the reservoir, another good place. As I got out of the car and wandered along the side of the reservoir for a few hundred yards in the warm sun two large birds of prey appeared above the forested hill on the other side of the water half a mile away. One disappeared almost immediately but the other circled round and round above the wood on still wings, soon joined by two buzzards. Goshawk! I had heard that they had been seen here and had fondly, but not optimistically, hoped that I might find them. The bird, big, broad-winged and bulky, like an oversize sparrowhawk, kept circling for a couple of minutes or more and eventually disappeared behind the hill in a long shallow glide, speed and power personified.

A small party of redpolls feeding acrobatically on

Redpolls by the reservoir

SPRING scene on previous pages shows blackcaps, male chaffinch, female mallard and ducklings, and a willow warbler.

the birches alongside the reservoir edge provided a further diversion, but the stony shores held nothing but two or three pied wagtails.

Once more I moved on and into the next valley. Here a lovely party of nine goosander rippled the calm water on the reservoir where it was black under the reflection of the opposite hillside. These elegant diving ducks, the males so strikingly black and white at a distance (although the 'black' head is in fact a deep bottle-green at close quarters), are recent additions to our list of breeding birds in Wales, having extended their range southwards from Scotland and northern England. Within minutes of leaving the goosanders there were two kites circling above the head of the valley and a third one cruising low over

the steep fields beyond the wood. Like the goshawks, these were indeed red-letter birds, although not unexpected: they can be seen here regularly in winter and early spring. It was one of those warm, welcome March days which do so much to alleviate the tail-end of winter, one which seems to be too good to be true. All the birds you hope for actually appear and a lone peregrine cruising lazily over the valley just before I left scarcely surprised me by this time. Finally the wheatear eventually turned up too: as I left to return home I caught the flash of white in the corner of my eye and quite suddenly he was there, a bold herald of early spring, standing as always in the open, conspicuously perched on top of the low stone wall at the roadside.

THE HERONRY

On the other side of the main road at the bottom of our lane there is a small heronry of six to eight pairs each year. They nest in company with some rooks in a line of tall hedgerow oaks on the top side of an ancient river terrace along the River Severn, which flows two hundred yards away across the valley floor.

Although it is only a small heronry it gives us a lot of pleasure during early spring before the leaves obscure the nests, by which time they are already full of growing youngsters. We slow down on the school run each morning to do an almost ritual count of the herons at the nests. Herons are peculiar birds, in several ways. Once the young have fledged in June the heronry is totally abandoned until the following February or March; unlike the nearby rooks, which pay regular visits to the rookery, the herons never make even cursory visits until the time comes to

repair the nests again. However, once spring is close, an interesting phenomenon occurs during the weeks leading up to the reoccupation of the nesting trees. From time to time in late February – varying from year to year according to the weather – individual birds begin to visit the long field near the heronry, where they stand about for hours on end apparently doing nothing: it is a strange, static ceremony with no obvious explanation. The birds congregate in the same field each year and their numbers build up modestly over the period – the week or two immediately before the birds go back up to their tree-top nests. This inert gathering is somewhat akin to a daytime roost, although just occasionally a new arrival lands with open wings and performs a brief skipping run which itself stimulates one or two of the other birds to do the same. It is an odd and somewhat undignified performance for a normally dignified bird, but it is all over in a second or two and the silent roost resumes.

The reason for this strange ritual is obscure. It is spasmodic and seldom, if ever, develops into anything overtly sexual. Most likely it is to do with the birds being drawn towards the colony for breeding but having to wait to attain the right physiological state before they join the colony again as one of the breeding birds. Also at this time, for a few brief weeks, the birds suddenly develop much redder bills and eye rings which are distinct through binoculars at reasonably close range. They lose these bright colourings again once pairing and mating are complete and egg laying is under way.

We think of these birds, patronizingly, as being 'our' herons; several individuals make regular use of the brook outside the house or fly ponderously overhead to stalk the little moorland pools and bogs on the hills above for frogs, voles or newts.

Herons

Neck drawn back in flight –
slow wing beats.

Male's 'stretch display'
guards the nest.

Male's threat
posture at the nest.

Herons congregating in the field
near the heronry. Sometimes one breaks into
a skipping run, with wings spread.

CHIFFCHAFFS

The earliest mistle thrushes have been nesting for a week or two by mid-March, and so have the ravens in the hills. Although we recognize these happenings as manifestations of spring, the over-wintering flocks of wildfowl in the river meadows taking sanctuary from the frozen waters of eastern and northern Europe are still intact, even if their numbers are visibly smaller than they were three weeks ago; the riverside meadows, too, are full of fieldfares, who have not yet considered making their move to the north to breed. Nevertheless, surely the real signs of strengthening spring are with us now?

The early light of morning brings with it a distinct impression of bird chorus in the garden. The mistle thrush sings stridently from the top of a tall fir tree and two robins can be heard from fairly high up too, one from the top of the rhododendrons and the other from the higher branches of one of the big wild cherry trees by the brook. Robins frequently sing from higher up in the early part of the season, as if to proclaim tenure of their springtime territory. Afterwards they retreat closer to ground-level, where they posture and sing to defend the area against rivals. Lusty spasms of song from a male wren temporarily dominate the chorus and a blackbird produces some richly mellow phrases, but this only happens as yet on the really fine mornings and seems to lack real enthusiasm.

Song is characteristically a talent restricted to male birds. It is therefore an additional aid to identifying individuals within species such as song thrush or blue-tit where the plumages are indistinguishable. None the less there are outstanding exceptions (the robin, for example), most frequently in those birds which need to defend individual territories throughout the year. The most important function of song is to advertise the occupancy of the singer's territory and thereby warn off others of the same species. As spring advances and the male needs to seek a partner the singing fulfils a dual role, also advertising the male's availability. Once the pair is formed and the territory established the boundaries must be maintained by the male to ensure a sufficient food supply for the family. In pursuit of this aim, song is the most important

Chiffchaff

Wren

weapon in the male's repertoire: the only additional actions available to him are posturing and occasional skirmishes with the boldest or most persistent of would-be interlopers.

There may be plenty of time yet for more hard weather: these first suspicions of spring are still tenuous. One very welcome sign, however, is the sound 'chiff, chaff, chiff, chiff, chaff, chiff, chaff'. The first chiffchaff of spring always makes my heart miss a beat. Some years the suddenness of the soft, insistent call almost makes one jump, while in other years it seems to arrive more by stealth: slowly one realizes that there is a chiffchaff calling somewhere amongst the chattering of the brook and the other general background noises. They arrive early for insect-eating birds, improbably far in advance of most of the other insectivores. This March has been so cold and inhospitable most of the time that I wonder how they make ends meet.

As a slightly strange corollary to these traditional and encouraging signs of spring, there is an old buzzard which roosts in the steep oakwood across the lane and puts in a regular early-morning appearance. Buzzards, like other birds of prey, are not notable for their early rising but prefer to emerge when the sun has started to heat the air and they can make use of the rising warmth. This one, however, emerges daily from the wood well before light, circles round calling plaintively, silhouetted against the lightening night sky, then glides away over the fields down the narrow valley. I have failed to find a convincing explanation for this somewhat abnormal behaviour and can only presume that the buzzard has lighted on a profitable early-morning source of food (possibly moles, for although they are popularly thought to be unpalatable to birds buzzards will certainly take them when they are available).

And how bright the blue-tits and great tits begin to look! This is no illusion, for they are indeed smartening up for courtship and will be brighter and more assertive over the next few weeks than at any other time of year.

This subtle but marked change of plumage is achieved not by moulting (their one annual moult occurs in the summer after breeding) but by the simple expedient of abrasion, whereby the duller tips of the feathers are gradually worn away through the winter, starting to reveal the brighter colours of spring just at the right time. By this means the blue-tits become bluer and the black bellies of the great tits become broader and blacker. By April they will be at their expansive best.

THE GREBES OF EBYR

In the whole spectrum of springtime courtship in our native birds, no courtship display is more fantastic and beautiful than that of the great crested grebes.

In much the same way as song takes on an enhanced role in the process of pairing and partner selection, so does courtship become increasingly important. Not only must the male attract a partner, but having done so he must maintain and strengthen the pair bond through the season of reproduction and must achieve the ultimate function of mating. In all these respects the vigour and potency of the male's display, be it elaborate as in the case of the grebes, seemingly indifferent as in that of spotted flycatchers, or colourful as in peacocks, is of crucial importance in the process of successful reproduction.

Great crested grebes have done well in recent years and breed commonly on lowland lakes and gravel pits in England; in Wales, where there is not much lowland, they are less plentiful but a couple of pairs nest on Llyn Ebyr, a quiet, reed-fringed lake surrounded by woodland deep in the foothills of the upper Severn valley a mile or two from home. Look for displaying grebes early in the spring, for they are very early nesters and many, if not most, are on eggs well before March is out.

Several times I have been over to Llyn Ebyr on a fine day in March in the forlorn hope of seeing the remarkable and rare penguin-dance of the grebes; like so many other naturalists, I have had no success to date. When I last visited, the pairs of grebes were at their respective ends of the lake. The nearer pair was close together preening when I arrived. Their erect crests and tippets were bright and prominent; we call it 'summer' plumage but they frequently develop it as early as December. What strange birds they are! Not only are they unique amongst our birds in the form of their decorative features but they have a most unusual shared behaviour in which none of the essential functions of courtship, display, territory defence or nesting are exclusive to one sex as they are in other species. The male and female are as alike as peas in a pod, with the result that you cannot even be sure which one does the soliciting: it is known for a fact that the female occasionally mounts the male! Their lifestyle is so complicated that I sometimes wonder if anyone knows for sure which one actually lays the eggs.

Before long I had been unconsciously distracted in my grebe-watching and was trying to locate woodland birds calling in the old alders behind me. When I picked up my grebes again they were offshore from their usual nest-site, swimming slowly towards each other with necks stretched high, swinging their heads rhythmically from side to side with their ruffs widely spread. A few feet apart now, they faced each other and shook their heads vigorously for a few seconds before breaking off and one after the other they stiffly turned their heads backwards momentarily to false-preen the feathers on their backs before facing each other for further head-shaking. It is a magical and arresting display and is the commonest of several very strange and distinctive courtship displays. Sometimes one is lucky enough to see them spread low on the surface of the water, facing each other with wings open and bent forward to reveal the fine wing patterns, and head drawn back with the tippets fanned wide.

Perhaps one day I will be lucky enough to see the spectacular 'penguin-dancing', wherein both birds dive and gather weeds underwater in their dagger bills, then rise, swim towards each other and indulge in a breathtaking dance, both birds rearing up out of the water and meeting breast to breast, keeping position by treading water furiously before they both subside again and swim away. For this day, however, I had to content myself once again with various bouts of head-shaking and several skirmishes with neighbouring coots.

Of all our native water birds great crested grebes are the most interesting. As well as their distinctive plumage, weird courtship and odd social life they have other peculiarities: their eggs are often incubated in nests of sodden weeds and therefore need specially thick protective layers of shell; they carry their young concealed on their backs and they feed them initially on small fish and feathers! The complexities of their existence make grebes the most intriguing, and attractive, members of our water-bird community.

Great crested grebes

Grebes' courtship –
birds swing their heads
from side to side
with ruffs widely spread.

'Penguin-dancing' –
the pair raise
themselves up,
face to face,
offering weed.

Low on the surface
with wings outstretched to show
their pattern.

False-preening
feathers on the back.

Neck on the water,
soliciting the female.

A female great crested grebe
on the nest with two striped chicks on her back.

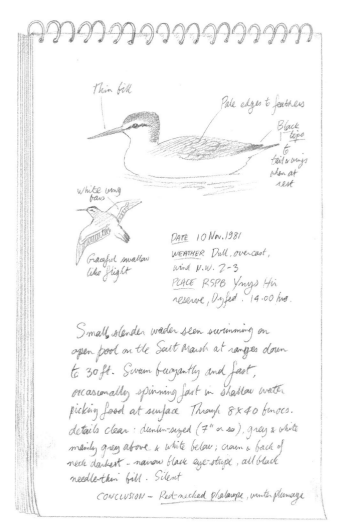

Thin bill

Pale edges to feathers

Black tips to tail & wings when at rest

White wing bars

Graceful swallow like flight

DATE 10 Nov. 1981
WEATHER Dull, overcast, wind N.W. 2-3
PLACE RSPB Ynys Hir reserve, Dyfed. 14.00 hrs.

Small slender wader seen swimming on open pool on the Salt Marsh at ranges down to 30 ft. Swam buoyantly and fast, occasionally spinning fast in shallow water picking food at surface. Through 8 x 40 binocs. details clear: dunlin-sized (7" or so), grey & white mainly grey above & white below; crown & back of neck darkest - narrow black eye-stripe, all black needle-thin bill. Silent

CONCLUSION - Red-necked phalarope, winter plumage

IN THE FIELD

Birdwatching is an interest anyone can take up, no matter where one lives, for there are birds everywhere, all the time. It has the great advantage over many pastimes of being immediately, easily and freely available to all, for it requires no sophisticated or expensive equipment – although as your interest grows you may well decide to invest in a pair of binoculars. Moreover, it spans all age-groups, from five to one hundred years, and it is enjoyable whatever one's level of knowledge or proficiency. Add to this the fact that an interest in birds soon produces the desire to visit places where special species can be seen (an activity which can be enjoyed by the whole family) and it becomes easy to understand why

birdwatching has become a major recreational activity in recent decades.

Many people derive their first pleasure from birds by simply watching them in the garden or the park. If a bird looks interesting, or amusing, is beautiful or impressive or is engaged in seemingly curious behaviour – or, perhaps, has an attractive song – these aspects can all be appreciated without any prior knowledge of their significance. None the less, knowing a little about what you are looking at will greatly enhance your enjoyment of birdwatching, so it is worth taking the trouble to sharpen up your powers of observation.

One way of doing this is to get into the habit of making notes, and sketching, birds you see. The example illustrated here highlights not only the features of the bird that you should be observing (size, coloration, features, behaviour, including style of flight and other forms of locomotion, feeding habits, call or song – or lack of them), but one or two essential ancillary factors: the date, the place, the time and a note of the climatic conditions prevailing when you saw the bird.

Keeping such a notebook means you will eventually have built up a useful record of your observations, and it will also help to improve the accuracy with which you keep the notes and make the sketches. In these ways your experience and skill in identification will develop rapidly and you will be much better equipped to recognize the important features of rarer, or more unusual, birds when they occur.

Binoculars, one of the birdwatcher's basic items of equipment, should be chosen carefully: select a pair for ease of handling, smooth focusing and suitable weight, as well as for magnification and manufacturer. Beware of cheap or secondhand pairs unless you have tested them carefully. The specifications, e.g. 8 × 30, 8 × 40 or 7 × 50, indicate firstly the magnification, secondly the size (in millimetres) of the front lens. For woodland or general use choose something like an 8 × 40 pair. Larger specifications, such as 10 × 50, can be limiting as they are usually heavy and tend to magnify haze, but they are useful for seawatching.

Birdwatching can mean looking at birds through a window, walking the countryside with binoculars or making a special trip, perhaps out to sea or to a nature reserve, to see certain species. In many situations a car can provide an excellent hide and will often allow close-up viewing, especially if you use a 'wait-and-see' technique: park, or sit, in a promising spot and wait for the birds to reveal themselves (above the high-tide mark on an advancing tide is a good place to wait, for the birds will be pushed towards you by the rising water). Silence and stillness are vital in most birdwatching situations, especially when watching birds at close range or when using the 'wait-and-see' method, so children and dogs must be controlled.

When watching in the open, as opposed to using a hide or car, try to have the sun behind you, otherwise you will be handicapped by not being able to see the colours and other details of the birds and will have only their silhouettes from which to identify them.

Station yourself against a background if watching at close quarters, but remember the risks of unwittingly keeping birds off their nests and causing them to desert, or of allowing predators to reach nests. Be aware of birds' alarm and distress calls and move on at once if your presence seems to be upsetting them. Avoid, too, treading on the nests of ground-nesting species yourself.

If you visit one of the many nature reserves around Britain, notably RSPB ones, you will find well-situated hides allowing easy access to birds without disturbing them and providing outstanding close-up views of many species which would otherwise be difficult to approach.

×7　　　　　×8　　　　　×10

When choosing binoculars check that the focusing wheel moves freely; that the cross-piece joining the eye-pieces is fairly rigid and not warped, and that the body is sound. Make sure that the lenses are coated — they should have a uniform blue tinge. Also check for flaws or dirt on their surfaces. Never touch the lenses with your fingers.

The field of view decreases with increasing magnification. 8× magnification is ideal for most purposes.

8×40

LAPWINGS

No sight or sound is more evocative of spring than the frenzied aerial displays and abandoned 'singing' of the lapwing, the most widespread and familiar of all our plovers. From the flat coastal salt marshes and the low river meadows, across the open chalk downs of southern England and up into the hills of northern England and Wales and the islands of Scotland the lapwings spread their universal spring message of joy throughout March and April.

They first appear on the breeding areas as early as February having broken away from the big winter flocks, and they will spend a month or so pairing, setting up territory, displaying and filling the spring air with wild screaming before the first eggs appear at the end of March. During this time the stormy uncertainties of March will drive them off the hills and downs again, sometimes for days at a time. This year the more violent moods of March recurred time after time with periods of fierce wind and torrential rain. These wild days of March tossed the black-headed gulls about like confetti as they gathered into flocks on the flooded pastures in the valley before moving up to their peaty pools and small lakes in the nearby hills. The innumerable flooded pools in the fields provided rich feeding at such a time as the soil invertebrates were flushed to the surface, and the lapwings joined with the gulls to share in the orgy of food – convenient timing this year, just when the females needed to be in the peak of condition to form the eggs inside them.

During the milder and calmer intervals, and especially as March progresses, the lapwings spend more and more time in the breeding fields. They are often in loose colonies of several pairs or more, rather than scattered singly, and steadily the displaying and song-flighting increases in intensity. No other British bird has a flying display which is more exuberant and spectacular than the frenzied tumbling song-flight of the male lapwing. After take-off it quickens its flight on broad, rounded wings and shoots upwards thirty feet or more almost vertically before cascading headlong earthwards in a wild twisting, tumbling fall. It pulls out of it to shoot up again when only feet from the ground and repeat the display. As it throws itself from side to side the black of its upper parts alternates with the white of the underside, like the flashing of a light against the dark sky above the hillside. Nor is this a silent display: it is accompanied by an equally wild evocative song, repeated 'pee-ah-weet, pee-ah-weet' and the pulsing throb of air through the widespread primaries.

On the ground males match up face to face, stretching high and stalking each other a few paces at a time in an endless but unresolved endeavour to agree their territories. The male makes several exploratory nesting scrapes, tilting forward on his breast and scraping backwards with his feet. At the height of his intensity he will scrape vigorously time after time, even when no female is immediately close by. His energy and enthusiasm will attract a partner in the end. He tempts the female to interest herself in him with much bowing, flicking of the black and white tail and quiet calling; she will join him in the scraping and there will be much tossing of grasses and posturing as the bond between them is forged. The male displays his fine chestnut undertail feathers to the female by facing away, pointing his head down and lifting his tail high – the immodest can-can dancer.

Until the passing of the Wildlife and Countryside Act in 1981 it was still legal to gather lapwings' eggs for the table up to 15 April, but this anachronism has now been removed and the lapwing, now so much scarcer over much of Britain than in the last century (when eggs were collected in thousands), can now be spared that indignity.

Often in loose colonies
Lapwings indulge in
wild aerial displays.

The male displays
his chestnut undertail feathers
in courtship.

Two males
face up to each other on territory.

Lapwings

SWALLOWS AND MARTINS

One swallow doesn't make a summer, but the sight of them flicking over the fields again, hawking insects under the chestnut trees and flying in and out of the farm buildings, is as welcome as summer itself, even on a drab April day when they must find insects difficult to come by. By the middle of the month most of the resident birds are back, adults faithfully returning to the same outbuildings as last year after a seven-month absence which has taken them perhaps as far as Cape Province and back. By this time too the first house martins are back above the streets and roofs of a thousand cities, towns and villages, for they are one of our most attractive urban – as well as rural – birds.

The bulk of the martins arrive later than the swallows and for the first few days they often keep company with them, flying to and fro over the pools and river meadows where the greatest amount of insect food is to be found. It is some time before nesting will be fully under way for the martins, but a few are already starting to repair their nests and I watched three or four of them dropping down to a muddy farmyard gateway and collecting little gobbets of mud for their nests. They have an amusing nautical roll as they move about on the ground, lifting their bodies clear of the mud by stretching their inadequate legs and frequently assisting themselves by half-opening their wings. They carry each beakful of mud up to the nest, where they cling easily to the side of it and work the mud expertly and energetically into the shape of the nest. They are confiding at the nest and allow close approach. Their spring plumage is bright and fresh; they have glossy blue upper parts (although the wings are browner and duller), and pure white below, with the distinctive and familiar white rump. As they cling to the nest all the detail is clearly visible except for the little dark eye which is so often hidden behind the line of the blue-black cap.

A few days after the birds had been collecting their mud I witnessed a pathetic and sad little incident. As I drove round a corner of the main road nearby I saw a house martin sitting in the middle of the road ahead of me. This was unusual enough in itself, but there seemed something else strange about it too. As I approached the bird rose, circling round and calling repeatedly, and I realized that it had been sitting on the dead body of another martin, presumably its mate,

still warm and apparently hit by a passing car. It is foolish to ascribe human emotions to birds or other animals, but by the pathetic way in which the bird continued to fly round near the little carcass, calling all the time, there was no doubt whatsoever in my mind that it was fully conscious of the loss – or at least the ill-fate – of its partner. None the less a small bird's memory must be short and it would probably fine another mate very quickly at this time of year.

We associate both swallows and house martins with human habitations during the time they are with us in the summer but of the two it is the martin which is particularly linked with houses; if swallows are the birds of barns and other outbuildings it is the martins which rely on the eaves of our houses, almost without exception, for nesting. They suffer plenty of competition for the nests they have built themselves in previous years, mainly from house sparrows – which, as resident birds, start the season with the

Sparrow at house martin's nest

advantage of being on site and nest-building before the martins are even in the country. The sparrows can oust them if they wish in any case, but we can actively help to prevent such takeovers by hanging weighted strings or the like in front of the nests to deny the sparrows the horizontal approach to the nests which they need (martins fly up to the nests from below).

Occasionally bridges make popular alternative nesting-sites and there is one colony on the older of the two bridges over the Severn at Atcham in Shropshire of which I am particularly fond. It was the largest colony in the country at one time, rising to about 335 nests in the 1960s, but has declined again since then. I notice that the martins never seem to have problems from house sparrows there – presumably because the sparrows do not relish being perched precariously over the swirling river.

NESTING

One of the archetypal signs of the approach of spring is the sight of wrens exploring for nest-sites amongst the exposed roots of brookside trees and around the woodsheds. The cock birds have a busy time immediately ahead of them, not only establishing and protecting a territory but also building a selection of nests from which the female will eventually select one to line and use. Blue-tits, too, are taking steps towards setting up home. A male bird is paying tentative visits to a couple of nest-boxes on trees but is also critically examining a hole in the brickwork of one of the outhouses, where a pair of great tits nested successfully last year.

The jackdaws, beautiful and intelligent birds, are making a nest deep in one of the chimneys, which is not entirely to our liking. They are among the first to take advantage of the many nesting materials we have put out once they have blocked the chimney with their sticks and are ready to line the nest. If we fail to put out material they explore the stable for pony hairs and threads of discarded baler twine. Occasionally they even sit on the pony's mane or the sheeps' backs and help themselves.

Almost all birds, the world over, lay and incubate their eggs in nests, and the nests they build vary a great deal in their complexity, size and shape. Some opt for a rudimentary 'scrape' on the ground; some lay their eggs in wholly unprepared sites, which could,

Jackdaws scavenging for nesting material

The hen selects a nest
from several built by the cock
and lines it with feathers.

HOUSE MARTIN

House martin
build their
mud cups under e

WREN

House martins gathering mud for their nest.

GOLDCREST

The goldcrest's nest
is a tiny hammock
of mosses and gossamer.

LONG-TAILED-TIT

A delicate dome of
lichens, hair and webs
lined with innumerable feathers.

The nest is built of twigs, grasses and moss
with a hard lining of mud.

SONG THRUSH

SWALLOW

Swallows build in outhouses,
their nests untidy cups
of mud and grasses.

CHAFFINCH

The willow warbler's domed nest,
hidden in vegetation at ground level.

An immaculate nest
woven of cobwebs, roots,
mosses and lichen.

WILLOW WARBLER

none the less, in a fairly loose interpretation, be termed a nest. Perhaps only parasitic birds, such as cuckoos, and several penguin species which incubate eggs between feet and belly (often moving considerable distances during the incubation period) can be said to use no nest-site whatever.

Birds, together with their eggs and young, are particularly vulnerable during the breeding season. They must employ either colonial strength, inaccessibility, physical presence or disguise to ensure the safety of their clutch.

Many bird species make little or no attempt at actually *building* nests, especially those birds which lay in the open on cliff ledges or on the ground, or in the recesses of burrows and holes in trees. Apart from these families the majority of British birds make more or less elaborate structures employing a wide variety of materials: for example, sticks, grasses, leaves, water vegetation, animal hair, lichens, feathers, cobwebs, saliva and mud. Some may be of enormous size – a raven's nest used year after year can reach six feet or more in height and as much in girth, and although they are constructed by only feet and bill, and in a very short time, they can be amazingly durable: rooks' nests will survive tree-top gales from one year to the next.

Of all bird groups it is the passerines, that huge order of perching birds (including crows, dippers, swallows and all the families of our familiar song birds), which make the greatest variety of nests. Each one is built to the pattern best suited to the needs of the species, that each bird knows through inherited instinct, using materials selected for maximum efficiency and, where applicable, camouflage and insulation.

NEST-BOXES

Placing nest-boxes at strategic points in your garden will help you to attract, in particular, blue-tits, great tits, nuthatches or even tree sparrows and pied flycatchers, depending on where you live.

Nest-boxes can be bought from RSPB outlets, garden centres or shops, which stock everything from conventional box-shaped models to more exotic ones that would be appropriate company for concrete gnomes, goblins and mushrooms. Alternatively, you can make your own.

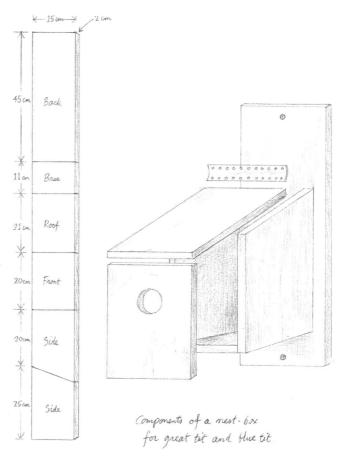

Components of a nest-box for great tit and blue tit

The main requirements of a nest-box are that it should be of about 4 × 4 inches internal area with a circular hole on one side at least 5 inches off its floor. A sloping roof with an overhang – removable if you want to be able to look inside – will ensure that the rain does not run into the box.

The size of the hole is critical: 1⅛ inches diameter will admit the small garden birds and still exclude house sparrows and starlings, which are the birds most liable to take over the boxes.

A plain wooden box, using wood that is ¾-inch thick, is the easiest type to make, but less conventional ones I have seen have been made of off-cuts of 4-inch plastic drainpipes from a local builder's yard, with wooden tops and bases made to fit; these are almost everlasting and wholly waterproof whilst being perfectly acceptable in appearance.

The box shown here is a conventional model, but there are other designs which accommodate more specialized requirements. For example, artificial house martin nests are obtainable: these are very effective and can often be instrumental in persuading the martins to start a new colony. Much larger nest-boxes along the lines of the conventional one described above are good for jackdaws, tawny owls and stock doves (but also starlings), while a popular open-fronted one is ideal for robins, spotted flycatchers and pied wagtails. However, my personal experience with the latter has been that only the flycatchers take to them readily.

Once you have your nest-box, you must site it carefully. Avoid places where the rain can collect in it

An old chimney-pot or a piece of drainage pipe makes an ideal nest for owls

Robin on an open-fronted nest-box

autumn or winter, which you should bear in mind before siting it in too awkward a position.

Try to put up your new boxes well in advance of the season so that the creosote is thoroughly dried and the birds can familiarize themselves with them in good time.

You can further encourage the birds to nest near you if you put out dispensers of nesting materials such as feathers, dog or cat combings, sheep's wool, cotton waste, horsehair, flock, hay and similar materials. None of these will be shunned, and could result in some highly decorative, if unusual, nests in some of your nest-boxes later in the season.

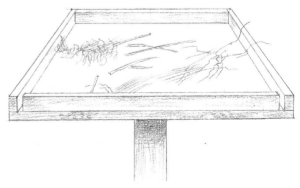

Birds will always make use of nesting material left out for them

or where rain can enter the hole direct; make sure it is not too low and if possible that it is out of the way of both cats and small boys. Once fixed in position, the box, if it is made of wood, will occasionally have to be treated with creosote or other preservative during

PIED FLYCATCHERS

Several pairs of attractive little pied flycatchers use the nest-boxes in our garden, along the stream and in the steep oak wood. They are probably the easiest of all hole-nesting birds to attract into boxes, although they have a strange and unexplained irregular distribution in western and northern Britain which excludes them from most of southern England. The female is a skewbald version of the pied male, one of the prettiest and liveliest of our summer visitors. The males arrive several days in advance of the females and immediately sing energetically as they fly from box to box staking out a territory and resolving differences with the local blue-tits and great tits. They are mostly in position by the time the females arrive to confirm the choice of a nesting-box. The males sing an attractive jingle of notes and accompany the females on the inspection of nest-boxes with much alarm calling and wing flicking.

'Pied' is a thoroughly appropriate name for this little bird, but I sometimes wonder whether 'spectacled flycatcher' would not be an even more descriptive name, as the two white patches on its forehead look for all the world like a diminutive pair of pince-nez and are one of its most distinctive features. Throughout the spring and early summer these delightful little birds grace our small valley and a thousand other similar valleys in Wales and the Marches until, come the end of June when the young leave the nest, they all vanish from view almost overnight. They will be there somewhere in the tops of the dense canopy of woodland, but silent and invisible to all.

THE RED KITES OF MID-WALES

The history of the guarding of red kite nest-sites is one of the classic stories of bird protection in these islands. It covers some eighty years so far and is certainly the longest-running annual nest-protection scheme. Each year a dedicated band of people – farmers, foresters, amateur naturalists, policemen, paid wardens, schoolteachers and other volunteers from various parts of the country – provides a network of protection for the nesting pairs.

One of my duties as an RSPB officer is to help look after the few remaining pairs of red kites. Like many others of our large birds of prey the story of these magnificent birds is a sad one of human persecution and extinction: there were once a large number of birds but in England they were finally shot out of existence around 1870 and in Scotland the gamekeeper's gun and trap allowed them only a further ten years. By the turn of the century only in the fastness and inaccessibility (in those days) of the Welsh hills were a few pairs managing to survive.

Over the years the enormous effort made to protect the birds has helped them build up from two or three pairs to about forty at present. One of my jobs early each year is to relocate each of these pairs. Much information comes in automatically from farmers and landowners but there are always difficult pairs which move a mile or more from last season's site and need to be searched out again – exciting work often done early in the mornings or in the evening.

One pair this year proved particularly elusive. I visited several farms and began to piece together a

The red kite at home
in the valleys of central Wales.

A kite at her wool-lined nest
in an oak tree feeds her two young.

Red kites

picture: the two birds had certainly been around at the end of March but had not been seen in the immediate area for two weeks or more, save for the occasional appearance of the male on the northern side of the valley. I would have to look further afield and it should clearly be in that area first. I tried again the next evening and searched several side valleys but with no success; not so much as a glimpse.

The third visit was more promising. I spoke to a farmer on a small, isolated farm who told me that he had seen the pair regularly around an old oak wood in a fold in the hills and pointed me in the right direction. It was just the information I had been waiting for, so I climbed the hillside with rising hope.

Red kites are magnificent birds at any time – indeed, I believe they are the most beautiful and graceful of all European raptors. Although I have seen them many times now, both perched and in flight, they are first and foremost birds of the air. When I visualize them they are always on the wing. They fly buoyantly with much lazy circling, gliding and slow wing-flapping, holding their long wings characteristically flexed, in a completely different fashion from that of the smaller, stiff-winged buzzards which are so much a part of the same countryside. For such large birds red kites are very agile and dexterous; they can, for example, weave in and out of the trees

in the nesting woods with impressive agility. The long, flexuous tail is employed constantly for balance, banking and turning.

However many times I see red kites, they never fail to quicken my pulse. The scene as the wood came into view did just that. It was an idyllic spot. A dilapidated oak wood perhaps some four acres in extent, with one or two ancient larches in it, hung on the far hillside, and above it rose a bank of yellow gorse and the flattened browns and sepias of last year's bracken. It was a compact and intimate scene. Linnets and a bright male stonechat were singing on the tops of gorse bushes beside the old track I was following, while a hovering kestrel high above the hill-top, tired of being pestered by the neighbourhood crows, moved away along the skyline.

But all this was only the colourful backdrop for the principal characters, for two magnificent kites, well conscious of my presence and already responding to it with occasional high-pitched mewings, wheeled back and forth across the meadow and over the straggling oak wood. At times one of them would fly almost below eye-level as they passed low in front of the wood. They moved with an enviable ease and mastery, the rich russet of their bodies and tails and their flecked white heads confirming them once more, in my mind, as the most beautiful birds of prey.

I searched the wood keenly through binoculars looking for the flat, bulky nest which clearly should have been there. Satisfied that I could distinguish it from the ruins of former crow and buzzard nests, I paused only long enough to take in the sight of the two beautiful wheeling birds again and then left them in peace. Another of this year's difficult pairs had been located and my task was done.

OSPREYS

The gracious and striking osprey was eliminated from the list of our breeding birds in the early years of this century by the keeper's gun and trap, and finally through the insatiable greed of Victorian egg-collectors and taxidermists. Only in the more enlightened times since the Second World War has it regained a toe-hold in the Highlands of Scotland, where the numbers have steadily risen to twenty or so pairs and the birds are assiduously protected by both the landowners and the RSPB. At the viewing facilities provided at Loch Garten in Speyside as many as 100,000 people have travelled to watch the birds in a single year.

Now, each spring ospreys pass northwards across England and Wales and may turn up in April or May over any lake or reservoir from the south coast of England to the meres of Cheshire, the reedy broads of East Anglia and the wide rivers of Wales or the Lake District. Ospreys are fish-eating birds of prey, perfectly adapted for taking live fish from the surface waters. The osprey's plunge to take a fish is awe-inspiring in its force and speed as the bird locates its prey, checks its flight and drops in a twisting dive or in a fast, planing glide. At the last moment it thrusts its feet ahead of it to hit the water – and the fish if it is successful – with a great splash. It rises, phoenix-like, from the water with ease, the fish firmly grasped in its strong, sharp talons; the feet are provided with special spiny soles and even a fully reversible toe to ensure that the writhing fish is held firm once it is caught.

After the breeding season is over in Scotland or Scandinavia the ospreys fly south again to winter in the warmth and easy living of the waters of the African coast.

Osprey

Mistle-thrush

THE QUICKENING PACE OF SPRING

As April slides quietly into May the fullness of spring is still to come. This is certainly so in the hills and valleys of my home in mid-Wales, where only the rhythmic swaying of emerald birches and the three-dimensional vividness of budding larch branches give real life or colour to the steep hillsides. It will be a week or more yet before the green haze of swelling buds on the oaks finally bursts into full and colourful newness and even longer before the grey ashes slowly begin to reflect the approach of summer. A strident mistle thrush swaying on the topmost twigs of the ash has already seen one nest emptied by the magpies and his partner now incubates the replacement clutch. His song is loud and challenging, and against the bare branches of the ash seems a throwback to the latter days of winter.

During April we phase out the winter feeding of birds at home. There are several schools of thought about this, but the one which has strongest currency is that it is probably best to run it down by mid-April and let the resident birds forage for all their own food as they establish pairs and set up territories prior to nest-building and egg-laying. Instead, we sometimes provide them with nest-building materials, for birds are more than willing to be helped in this way.

It seems a long time ago now that we clung to the first tenuous signs of spring, watched the ravens carrying sticks, searched for March wheatears and were taken by surprise by the first chiffchaff singing in the garden; but there are still other arrivals to come. Blackcaps, and before them garden warblers, do not reach these valleys until May is ten days old or more. Swifts do not appear until early May: they fly screaming over the rooftops and round the town buildings, sweep up and under the eaves and cling

Willow warblers skirmishing

32

briefly to the wall of last year's nest entrance before dropping off again and joining the other arrivals. Their all-too-brief stay with us in the summer brings with it an electrifying atmosphere. Whinchats are seen soon after the swifts, but it will be another week before the first spotted flycatchers – last of all the arrivals – finally return. None the less throughout the past weeks the rolling tide of spring bird arrivals has continued to build up. Many more willow warblers,

Swifts
prospecting for nests

Spotted flycatcher

chiffchaffs, whitethroats, turtle doves, redstarts, swallows, wheatears and tree pipits swell the numbers of the earlier arrivals and the countryside is alive with birds. Many of these are filling vacant territories but others are passing on to places further north, some of them a long way further.

It is relatively easy to feel the pulse of this migration. Every morning at this time of year I spend time in the garden before the family is up and quickly get to know the layout of the different territories for each species simply by noticing where each of the male birds concentrates his singing. On the rough bank beyond the hedge a willow warbler has been singing lustily since the third week of April and clearly has a mate, a territory and a nest; another pair is well established on the edge of the wood across the paddock and a third pair is building a nest in the thick bed of last year's uncut grass at the bottom of the orchard. Some mornings, however, there is a fourth

bird singing: once in the rhododendrons by the stream, a few days later another one in the boughs of the silver birch above the brook. If the stranger approaches too close to the established tenancies of the others there will be a brief singing duel and if necessary a short skirmish and chase which will repulse the interloper to a more respectful distance. It is not the same bird each time, neither are any of them trying to settle here – firstly, because the suitable sites around the garden are already taken, and also because these birds are an irresistible part of the rolling tide of migration, driven by a stronger imperative – they must go on, northwards! Occasionally one of these transitory willow warblers is visibly different from the others, distinctly browner above and whiter below than our usual olive-and-

Whinchat

Grey wagtail

yellow birds and almost certainly heading for
Scandinavia to breed, although a few of the ones that
stay in Scotland are also of this duskier morph.

It was exciting to watch one of these northern birds
early in the morning one day at the beginning of May,
as it foraged feverishly among the filigree twigs and
emerging leaves of the silver birch, pausing every so
often to produce a body-shaking burst of song. As I
marvelled once more at the minuteness of the body
which had taken it from Scandinavia to West Africa
and back I was reminded of one I had caught in a mist
net some years before in another garden. I had put a
tiny numbered aluminium ring on its leg – SE 15961 –
and wished it well as I released it. Twelve months and
heaven-knows-how-many-miles later the same bird,
still wearing its tiny ring, was hanging gently in the
net again in exactly the same spot in the garden – a
demonstration not only of the durability of such a tiny
9-gram frame (at least its second return journey from

Africa to the north) but also of the fineness of timing
and the amazing consistency of route which some
individual birds will follow.

GARDEN MIMICS

At this time of year it becomes almost justifiable –
certainly understandable – for a man to happen to be
just out of earshot of the normal hubbub and demands
of domestic life much of the time in deep and solitary
appreciation of the pulsing activity of insect, plant
and bird life. Such a place is given to me in the
sanctuary of the little orchard, nicely out of sight of
the house, where the stream bubbles past over the
rocks. Dippers, everlastingly bobbing, true to their
name, their dark, dumpy forms quickly revealed by
gleaming white chests; elegant, long-tailed grey
wagtails work their way up the brook and pied

flycatchers nest in a box on the oak tree. Half an hour's solitude here can produce the sights or sounds of thirty or more different bird species. It is a good place to be: a place where one can bare one's soul to oneself and think of either nothing or everything, at the same time remaining unconsciously alert to anything unusual or noteworthy that passes.

My selfish solitude was shaken one morning at the loud call of a buzzard not ten feet above the ground in the fir tree three yards behind me. I knew that my slightest movement would send him away, and I froze. Now buzzards are common in our area, gloriously common, but they are the sharpest-eyed of birds and such proximity was ridiculous. It called again and, after a short interval, again and again. I had never heard the call of a buzzard so near, so loud or so sharp. Out of the corner of my eye I watched a jay slide through the branches of the same tree, cross the brook and settle with satisfying solidity and a flick of the tail on the low branch of another fir. It called, stretching forward as it did so, not the strident raucous call of its family, but 'whoooo' and then 'ke-wick, ke-wick' – a perfect tawny owl! Not only had I been misled by the 'buzzard' but I had not realized until then what an accomplished mimic the jay can be; buzzard and tawny owl and I wondered what else was in its repertoire.

We know that a number of our passerine birds can be good mimics, starlings, skylarks and marsh warblers being among the best known, but I for one had no idea that the list included jay. Its normal voice is both limited and discordant, hence the sheer improbability of the impersonation.

Mimicry is a strange development of normal song, the bulk of which is learned from parents or others of the same species, and its purpose – for such there must be – remains obscure. The female partner (and neighbouring males) can recognize the individual song of a male and certainly the incorporation of 'borrowed' phrases from other species will heighten the individuality of a bird's pattern.

My experience of garden bird mimics was to be broadened even further the same month when – once again sitting in contemplation – the clear and unmistakable notes of a nightingale rang out from the shrubbery by the brook. Nightingale phrases they certainly were, but I knew that they were not emanating from an actual nightingale, firstly because the song consisted of a loose succession of individual

phrases strung together and interspersed with others, and secondly because nightingales do not reach this far north-west. The culprit turned out to be a blackcap, a particularly polished individual, who graced the garden with his rich song right through the summer. Once more I was left to ponder just how much there is that one does not know. That in itself seems a good enough reason to continue escaping to the sanctuary of the little orchard.

Blackcap

EXOTIC SPRING VISITORS

In this age of instant travel birdwatchers are one of those groups of people who have made telling use of the opportunities. The horizons of thousands of birdwatchers have dramatically, and quite literally, widened. Many of our friends had enthused about Morocco in spring and the thrill of seeing many of the amazing trans-Saharan migrants en route for our shores in the unreal context of dramatic African surroundings, so we decided to take a short break there.

I still find the rapid transportation from home to a place which until then has been a name familiar only from the atlas immensely exciting; when we found ourselves in the heat and brilliance of Agadir three hours after leaving bitter frost in Birmingham, our surroundings seemed unreal. We spent that night camped in the dunes outside the town on the edge of the Souss estuary and at first light we were up to explore the small, sandy inlet, well known to birdwatchers as a refuelling place for many shore birds on their journey north to Europe. In the outer part there was a dazzling flock of some three hundred flamingoes, with the huge Atlantic rollers behind giving the illusion of breaking on the sand bar many feet above them. Further in there were twenty-five spoonbills and the same number of little egrets rushing and darting in the shallow water in communal fishing; Kentish plovers were running all around us on the drier sand and mud. A party of sandwich terns were resting on a sand bar, still with a long way to go to north-west Europe, and there were one or two black-tailed godwits, a solitary greenshank, two spotted redshanks and a ruff.

We left the bustle of the coast and the Souss estuary for the next few days to travel deep into the interior, to the stony hills and oases of the Saharan fringes, where we expected the trans-Saharan migration of our northern breeding birds to be in full swing. We travelled, with frequent stops, enjoying the rich variety of Moroccan birds. On one stony desert plain we marvelled at the ritual dance of the huge houbara bustards in the first light of morning and watched the delicate, cream-coloured coursers running across the plains and merging with the background every time they stopped. Hoopoe larks were here too, large larks with black and white hoopoe-like wing pattern and marvellous song flight. The male was spiralling

upwards over the desert and then parachuting to earth, finally closing his wings and plummeting vertically for the last twenty feet or so at the end of a beautiful, fluty song. As well as many other larks and wheatears we saw a splendid lanner falcon which obligingly sat on a rock not a hundred yards from the roadside.

It was the isolated oases deep in the Saharan fringe that really captivated us, and amongst these we spent a couple of hectic days close to the birds – so familiar to us all at home – which had made the hazardous fifteen-hundred-mile crossing of the Sahara and many of which had several thousands of miles still to go. The wind had blown strongly from the north for the last day or two and must have taken a heavy toll on many individuals. We watched little parties of swallows, exhausted, sitting on boulders at the side of the road; some of them allowed approach within a few feet as we photographed them. In some of the oases, willow warblers and chiffchaffs moved lethargically through the palm fronds and among the waterside vegetation, already rebuilding their spent body resources.

On the side of one dry wadi a party of nine colourful rollers sat dejectedly, heads towards the strong wind, not moving as we walked close by them; in another wadi was a beautiful hoopoe and a small group of colourful bee-eaters. In one small Bedouin village we were befriended by the villagers, who insisted on taking us on a detailed tour of their cultivated patches, fish ponds and date palms, pointing out the various birds to us; one of the young village boys had a terrified woodchat shrike tethered and hanging loose by a coarse blade of grass threaded through the nostrils in its upper mandible. Thus maimed, it was used in conjunction with a spring-trap as a lure to catch other migrants destined for the pot. All these birds – roller, bee-eater, hoopoe and woodchat shrike – were particularly exciting for us. They occur only rarely on British shores, when they have overshot on their spring migration; just occasionally one will take advantage of an unusually warm summer to stay and breed. These are special birds for a British birdwatcher: rare and unusually colourful at home, but found here in profusion as we moved over the desert roads from one wadi to another.

In the tall grasses by one of the fish ponds was one solitary sedge warbler – the only one we saw throughout the whole trip. It is one more of the legion

Bee-eaters,
most colourful of spring
vagrants.

The roller is
a trans-Saharan migrant
and a rare straggler to Britain.

Hoopoes occasionally
stay to breed.

Woodchat shrike—
wanderer from
the Mediterranean.

of small birds which make the huge crossing of the Sahara at one go. Having stored up body fat for the journey in the swamp margins of Lake Chad or the marshes of the upper Niger a bird of this size will lose between a quarter and a half of its body weight on the crossing. It will need to regain most of this before embarking on the next stages, which include the increasing uncertainties of the spring weather further north.

Not only did it give us a very strange feeling to find these birds in such unfamiliar surroundings, but it also conveyed graphically the immense achievement of the journeys that our summer visitors make before we become aware of them in the relative cosiness of the English countryside. It is all very well to read about migration in books or watch television programmes about it, but while the facts are incredible enough the flesh-and-blood reality of this annual miracle can only register when you witness eyeball to eyeball those who have just made crossings of such heroic distances as these birds have.

WILDERNESS AND DUNLIN

High spring is something of a hopeless season for naturalists. It is a time when so much is happening that one wants to be everywhere at once: the season of trying to find twenty-five hours in a day. I was determined that this spring I would somehow make the time to go up on to the high hills for one of the long evenings. I had meant to do so the past year or two but something or other had always prevented me. Amongst all the wild hill areas in Wales there is only one tract of land left which I believe can truly be designated wilderness. For me, wilderness has to have more than remoteness and loneliness: it needs emptiness and size. You have to be able to cross one horizon and find the same empty landscape the other side. Above all it must be a place without people, not simply today and yesterday, but every day; a place where, paradoxically, the sudden sight of someone else is so great a surprise that it confirms the state of wilderness. The one such remaining tract I recognize is in mid-Wales, a rolling series of plateau hills, of endless moor consisting of molinia grass, sphagnum-moss bog and dissected peatland. It is a gloriously lonely area inhabited only by the ubiquitous sheep and by meadow pipits, skylarks, dunlin, golden plover

and foraging carrion crows, ravens and red kites. On a perfect evening in late spring or early summer this is an idyllic place in which to spend time.

Leaving the car on the road, I walked westwards up the slope through the thick tangle of last year's bracken to the top of the first steep brow. I paused among the boulders on the excuse of watching a pair of wheatears which obviously had young in a nest nearby and then I walked on towards the next brow. A solitary buzzard and a pair of ravens crossed the hill behind me. This is meadow pipit country, grass moorland criss-crossed by sheep tracks, mile after mile of tough, unpalatable nardus and molinia grassland with sphagnum-moss bogs and rushy flushes in the folds of the hills, and nondescript little brown meadow pipits singing and calling everywhere – nothing else, just meadow pipits and occasional startled sheep. It took two hours to reach the moor I was heading for, a great wide area of dissected peat

A pair of wheatears

bog and heather ridges. Evening shadows were already lengthening by now and the air was still and warm even at 1400 feet. I sat and soaked up the view and the beautiful loneliness of the hills. To the south and east fold after fold of hills melted to a horizon where the most distant hills already merged with the evening mistiness of the sky. To the west the light was clear and I recognized the line where the hills dropped down to the coastal plain flanking Cardigan Bay.

To imagine the hills green and verdant in late spring at this altitude is to fail to understand them. New growth comes late in these hills and the expanse all around is made up of browns, yellows and ochres – all of it made golden by the lowering sun. The landscape reflects mainly last year's growth, relieved only by the white clumps of frothy cotton grass and the tiny bright flowers of tormentil.

As I sat and looked it was utterly silent, the sort of silence you can almost hear. A carrion crow made a half-hearted pass at a returning red kite a mile or more away to the north. The kite twisted dexterously and avoided the corvid with consummate ease. They continued their different ways in leisurely fashion. A meadow pipit started to call unseen from a patch of heather on a peat hag nearby – an insistent, nagging 'tisp' which becomes boring in no time and almost annoyingly spoilt the silence with its persistence. A solitary cock grouse appeared briefly above the skyline on the peat hag, called once and shook itself, pheasant-like.

The sun neared the horizon and at last I heard one of the sounds I had come to find. A soft, purring trill came over the moor and two or three hundred yards away against the dimming blue of the sky was the small, fast-flying dunlin rising, dipping and circling over the moor, engaged in the evening ecstasy of his daily song flight. I felt the welling satisfaction of one aim fulfilled. The dunlin trilled again and to my right

The hills of Central Wales.
In the vastness of the wilderness
few birds break the silence:
a single crow molests a
passing red kite; a dunlin
performs its trilling
song-flight
in the late evening.
Golden plover, with
bell-like calls
nest here close by the dunlins.

The meadow pipit
is the most numerous
bird in this countryside,
singing and
calling everywhere.

Skylark

another had also begun singing. Among the very smallest of our wading birds, they are also the most numerous in winter, when thousands of immigrants swell the resident numbers to prosper on the food-rich estuaries round our shores. Very few stay to breed on the Welsh hills and they seemed strangely incongruous here on the high hills so far from the coast, even in the smart black-bellied, chestnut dress of summer. Here in the deep remoteness of the wilderness it is no use trying to locate these little birds in the convenience of midday for they will elude you. They fly in the softness of evening and those who would experience the delight of singing dunlin on the moors must seek them in the golden light of sunset.

I sat and enjoyed the sound of the dunlin until stiffening limbs urged me to move. As I prepared to leave in the gathering dusk another call reached me, the bell-like, melancholy call of golden plover, black and gold – the brightest and best of moorland waders. I found the bird easily enough through binoculars, head and shoulders protruding above the short heather. It ducked down, ran a few yards and appeared again on another little eminence. It called and seemed to regard me quizzically. Just behind him I picked out a dunlin not four yards away, dark now against the fading gold of the moor. The golden plover and the plover's page: it was the first time that I had seen this sight and could fully appreciate the significance of the dunlin's long-standing nickname.

It took two hours to walk back to the car in the dark. I had been away for six hours. In that time I had seen only twelve different species and heard two others (curlew and snipe). One would probably have to work very hard to find many places in southern Britain where you can walk for six hours on a perfect evening in late spring and encounter only fourteen species. I add them up knowing that while I may forget the list in a short while I am unlikely ever to forget the time spent on the high moor, and the perfection of sharing half an hour of solitude with such birds in such surroundings.

GOLDCRESTS

Each lunchtime I cross the road from the office and wander through the park to where the River Severn curves through the town on its way towards the Shropshire border. This town park, like any other, is a constant source of satisfaction for a naturalist. I suppose it revolves round the realization that even in the heart of human habitation we can rely on finding ourselves – those who care to look and see – cheek by jowl with a great range of wildlife. The most casual passer-by in the park knows the blackbirds, grey squirrels, robins, woodpigeons, mute swans and jackdaws which are always present. Far fewer people appreciate the dippers that take a short cut across the bend of the river flying high above the park, or the nuthatches, tree creepers, four titmouse species, lesser spotted woodpeckers and collared doves which also flourish here. Foxes use the park at night, otters pass up and down the river right through the heart of town, bramblings feed on the beechmast with marsh-tits and chaffinches in the winter and a lone buzzard has lived here for a year or more. Sparrowhawks take advantage of the host of smaller birds: one even flew into the RSPB office window in the High Street one day, presumably seeking personal privilege. Town parks up and down the country all have similar riches, and right in front of our eyes, time after time, our towns and cities will reward the observant watcher.

They have planted a little row of Lawson's cypress by the entrance to the park to mask the brick and concrete pathways and in their own right these already contribute to the wider life of the park. The town sparrows flee into the adolescent branches as each pedestrian passes by to emerge again one by one within the minute; stinkhorns flourish each autumn in the rich soil under the trees and blackbirds roost in the dense greenery in winter.

A pair of goldcrests, at 7cm and 4 grams the tiniest of our birds (so minute they seem to be mere suggestions of life-size birds), have nested in one of these shrubby trees. The nest itself is an almost unbelievably delicate and yet resilient arrangement of cobwebs, mosses and lichens, lined with a mass of small feathers (where do so many birds find all the spare feathers to line their nests with?). It is slung hammock-like on cobweb handles under the shelter of one of the denser boughs and it was obvious from the parental excitement and activity one lunchtime that

momentous events were afoot. The first young brood
of the goldcrest season was ready to leave and indeed
one of the bolder (or imprudent) ones was already on
the ground below the nest – stumpy, flightless, minute
and ungraceful. I picked it up in the palm of my hand
as it continued to pour out the thinnest of insistent
hunger cries. The parents flitted agitatedly from frond
to frond three feet away. I held out my hand and at
last the female, torn between maternal duty and
prudence, could resist the calls no more. She flew to
my hand, settled and pushed an oak tortrix caterpillar
into the fledgling's gaping bill. After looking up and
staring me straight in the eye, she repeated the process
and then left. I returned her young one to the vicinity
of the nest and we each went on our separate ways
with our respective honour satisfied.

Now in the lengthening days of May grey wagtails
are nesting under the bridge, while the rookery round
the Town Hall is at full activity, rivalling the traffic
and the market for noise – and spraying the unwary
lunchtime picnickers below. The noisy mistle thrush
is in fact taunting the roosting tawny owl in the ivy on
an ancient oak above the old motte. It is something of
a ritual: the tawny owl sleeps there each day, the
mistle thrush knows it and each day goes through a
charade of rage. The tawny owl tries to ignore it,
sleeps, wakes up as the rooks are eventually
quietening down for the night and silently goes about
its nightly business.

Goldcrest feeding its young

PEREGRINES

The insistence with which peregrines have recovered from the depths to which the species plummeted in the 1950s and 1960s has been one of the recent phenomena of British wildlife; as well as the joy this brings to birdwatchers and conservationists it demonstrates too the amazing resilience some species and their unimagined ability to recover given adequate opportunity. In Wales the use of toxic chemicals left us with a legacy of a mere one or two pairs were there had formerly been a population of well into three figures. Since the most damaging chemicals were withdrawn the numbers have steadily recovered, gradually and painfully slowly in the first years of the early 1970s but almost at a gallop in the past two or three seasons. During the last decadal national survey of peregrines the RSPB in Wales had the responsibility of ensuring that every possible peregrine nest-site was visited at intervals during the season to ascertain whether the birds were breeding there or not. The experience left me with many memories and a feeling of deep privilege and satisfaction at having spent time in the close company of such a magnificent bird. The peregrine is all muscle and efficiency, a bird of awesome speed and power, striking its prey at the climax of a thunderbolt aerial stoop; it is probably the ultimate example in all the bird kingdom of the majesty of flight.

One particular memory concerns a site in the valleys of South Wales which I shall call Carreg yr Hebog (the falcon's rock). In its own right it was an atypical and slightly improbable site. To reach it I walked steeply uphill through a mile or more of dark

sitka forest with John Evans, a 14-year-old boy for whom life had taken on a different dimension since he had discovered these legendary birds on their crag here above his home valley the previous year. I prefer not to think what John's school attendance was like that May, but he was able to tell me almost hour by hour how the birds behaved each day: which one was incubating, when food was brought, where the male went to hunt, and what intruding kestrels and ravens had been driven away in a fury of aggression. He looked directly at the nest ledge from his home a mile and a half away on the other side of the valley and he lived that spring with the single-minded determination to protect the birds.

The dark forest paths gave way to the blinding light of early morning on the open hill. Above us were loose spoil heaps from old mine workings and above them on the crest of the valley side a line of crags which were typical of the upper reaches of many of the coalfield valleys. Behind us, beyond the forest and across the valley, were the smoke, the rhythmic hum and the terraced villages of industrial Wales: already this pair of peregrines had had its first clutch of eggs taken by boys from over the mountain.

Here above the forest edge it was quiet and beautiful. Young birches and sallows were established on the older spoil heaps with gorse and broom; a tree pipit was in full song all the time we were there, climbing steeply a hundred feet or more and

The stoop of a peregrine
to take a pigeon.

The young bird is
brown above and streaked below.

A female incubating on an old raven's nest.

The male peregrine is smaller and more compact
than the female.

Four fluffy eyasses,
fat and ungainly, wait on the nesting ledge.

parachuting down to the topmost twigs of birch, hawthorn or sallow. A willow warbler sang, and so did a wren, its disproportionate song reeling out from the rank heather and boulders at the base of the cliff; the cliff ledges were bright with woodrush, spangled yellow with tormentil and primroses, and with the fresh white umbels of flowers on rowan trees clinging to crevices on the cliff face.

We scrambled and slid up the side of the first spoil heap and stood at the base of the cliff. The rocks above us were dashed with whitewash. Thirty feet up was the great stick edifice of an old raven's nest and there in full view, seemingly an arm's length away, was a female peregrine, head inclined downwards gazing at us. Peregrines are unpredictable in their reactions to humans approaching their nests: some are reasonably placid and confiding, others notoriously edgy and easily disturbed. Never before had I been as close to a wild peregrine as I was to this one. She seemed wholly unconcerned by our presence, flicking her head from time to time to deter the flies that scavenged for scraps of meat on the rim of the nest. She took no notice when we used binoculars but tilted her head up once to watch as the male bird appeared over the cliff, called, banked and disappeared beyond the end of the crags in a steep slanting glide. The

peregrines had returned to the heart of Wales.

A week later the female peregrine was dead. She was shot on the nest, presumably by pigeon fanciers, and left there. She was too fearless and had no chance. Rumour has it that the male was also shot. When John realized something was wrong he ran there all the way. He climbed the cliff, foolhardy but brave – I could not have done so. One of the young had already starved; the other he put inside his shirt and saved. Three months later it flew to the wild again in mid-Wales and will doubtless return to the valleys in the fullness of time to take its chance.

I personally visited several other eyries that summer, in some cases to mark the young birds in the nest with numbered metal rings and enjoy with amused speculation the thought that a row of four rotund grey eyasses, squatting ingloriously on their haunches, could ever evolve into masters of the air. On at least one occasion I flinched when an adult flashed past the cliff in front of me and the air rushed through its stiffened primaries. I revelled in the sight of a pair of peregrines working in unison to take a pigeon which did not even know it had been hit when the female killed it. But from that year of the peregrine, no memory will linger as long as that of the peregrines on Carreg yr Hebog.

Peregrine with young in raven's nest

Cuckoo at dunnock's nest

CUCKOOS

No bird is more familiar, certainly by name and by call, than the common cuckoo, which breeds throughout the length and breadth of Britain and, indeed, the whole of Europe. Despite the annual, albeit inconclusive, contest to record the first cuckoo of the year, the great bulk of arrivals does not reach the south coast of Britain until the third week of April, after which the birds quickly spread throughout the rest of the country. From their first arrival the males sing to advertise their presence and attract a mate. On the lower land they occupy almost all types of countryside, but where I live in mid-Wales they are predominantly birds of the *ffridd* land, the steep bracken and gorse-covered sides of the hills, and the rough grassy slopes, dotted with hawthorns, on the upper slopes of the hills.

During May and June from before dawn each day the cuckoos sing. Later they display, striking fear into the hearts of protesting meadow pipits who will unwittingly, and unwillingly, act as hosts for these demanding parasites from the south. The singing continues through May and the first half of June until the female has completed her drawn-out laying season, which lasts as long as six or seven weeks. Egg-laying does not usually start until the cuckoos have

been here three weeks or so. For a parasitic bird like the cuckoo, the laying season is inevitably simultaneous with the successive layings of its host species. The cuckoo must lay only in nests where the host's clutch of eggs is incomplete and incubation has consequently not yet begun. Most species of birds lay their eggs in the early part of the day but the cuckoo, remarkable in so many different ways, chooses to lay its eggs mostly in the late afternoon, which gives it the advantage of ample daylight time in which to locate the desired nest. This also allows the cuckoo to maximize the opportunity of selecting a time when the host pair is absent from the nest. Unlike the small birds which it parasitizes the female cuckoo lays eggs at two-day intervals. Another remarkable fact is that when the eggs are laid they are already partly incubated to help ensure that they hatch in advance of the host's eggs.

It is now well known that the female cuckoos do not change from one host species to another, either within one season or from one year to another. They almost certainly remain specific to the same hosts all the time. Different individual females can therefore be attributed as meadow pipit-cuckoos, dunnock-cuckoos or reed warbler-cuckoos. Accordingly each female only lays one type of mimetic eggs, depending on the host she disadvantages, and she can only

produce eggs on a constant pattern year after year to match those of her particular host. The three species mentioned above are those most frequently parasitized in Britain, although there are others, such as pied wagtail and reed bunting, which are used less frequently. The selection of the dominant host varies across the cuckoo's European range and in other countries garden warblers, robins and shrikes are amongst those which are habitually chosen.

Once the young cuckoo is successfully hatched its first task is to empty the nest of other eggs or hatching young. It achieves this within the first two days – often only a few hours after it has hatched and dried – by the superhuman effort of shovelling them, balanced on a special depression in the middle of its infant back, over the rim of the nest; at this stage the baby cuckoo is still blind and naked, but unbelievably muscular. The obliging foster parent will even move aside if necessary, in response to the monster's wrigglings, to enable the young bird to complete its ejection task, simply watching unconcerned as the rightful eggs or young are tipped to the ground below.

Food competition thus removed, the infant cuckoo

grows at a great rate: it equals its foster parents' weight within three or four days. Its growth continues at this rate for the first two weeks as the adults work ceaselessly to satisfy its insatiable demands. Cuckoos fledge at about twenty days and in the final week growth slows down whilst feathers are being fully formed and the bird exercises and prepares for flight.

Although the youngster, stumpy, inelegant, large-headed and constantly squawking for food, is out of the nest, the foster parents' work is not finished. It will be a further two weeks before the black-and-brown-barred youngster, now at least recognizably cuckoo-shaped, will leave them in peace and work its way southwards. By this time the adult male cuckoos have long since left, setting off on their return migration by the end of June when their tasks of territory establishment and mating have taken place. The females, too, only linger long enough to carry out their protracted laying, build up their body resources again and then depart. So the young cuckoos, never having set eyes on another of their kind, set off solo on the long flight beyond the Sahara and into Southern Africa to a winter site pre-ordained only by instinct.

Cuckoos in flight,
hawklike with pointed wings

Juvenile in
red-brown plumage

Adult cuckoo calling.

The newly hatched cuckoo ejects
the meadow pipit's eggs
before they hatch.

The parent pipit feeds the young cuckoo
by standing on its back.

INSTANT POND, INSTANT BIRDS

We had the local JCB in during late spring to dig a pond in the paddock across the brook. At first it probably sounds a pretty eccentric thing to do in a part of the country which is not actually noted for its shortage of water at any time of year, either falling, running or standing. Certainly the Blaen-y-Cwm (head of the valley) farmer above us thought it hilarious, the more so when another neighbour told him we had done it 'to keep frogs in'.

In truth it is really not quite as eccentric as it seems. For a start, the far side of the paddock has always been hopelessly wet where the water seeps out of the bottom of the wood at the foot of the steep valley side; we would have had to do something about it in any case and this was a perfect opportunity to practise what I regularly preach and make a virtue of necessity by curing the wet area through making a pond and simultaneously encouraging the local wildlife. So many ponds – once almost prerequisites on most farms – have been filled in over the last few decades that many of the dragonflies, frogs, toads, newts, water beetles and pond plants are much scarcer than they used to be. It saddens me that my own children are not as readily familiar with all these creatures and plants as I used to be when I was small.

Many of us can make a real contribution to this aspect of conservation by creating our own ponds. I am lucky, perhaps, in that we have a bit of space around us and can make a relatively large one (ours is about 15 × 10 yards), but anyone with a garden, even of pocket-handkerchief size, can make their own scaled-down version. I have seen many garden ponds of three to four feet across (some concreted, others with polythene linings) which have been seething with pond life, from water boatmen to frogs and bathing birds.

Our pond was cut into the slope of the bank and therefore has a six-foot cliff on one side (will we ever lure the kingfishers to breed there?). It is sheltered by the wood on that side, too, and has a couple of mature hawthorns. I shall plant one or two alders on the edge and a few aspens near the other side. The remainder is open to the field and I shall keep it so to provide a flight line to the pond for mallard, heron etc. . . . The children are already abusing the pond by seeing if they can leap from the top of the cliff on to the island, but

Mark out the pond area with wooden pegs
and dig the hole
letting the sides slope.

Line with polythene sheeting
and secure the edges with large stones.

Cover the overlapping edges with soil
in which pond-side plants can be established.

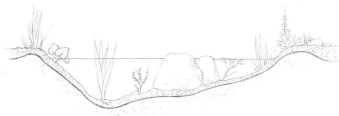

A successful pond will have plants
to oxygenate the water and some sort
of raised area on which the birds
can perch to drink and bathe.

they will tire of that before the pond is established.

The neighbours' Muscovy ducks appreciated my efforts immediately; they flew over the hedge and looked thoroughly at home on the pond within the day. This was a bit awkward because Muscovies are pretty voracious feeders and I watched one last year taking ten minutes or so to swallow a large, struggling frog, so I shall regard them with grave suspicion as the pond develops. A heron also found the pond very quickly but left after a brief examination had revealed its present sterility, but the pied wagtails already love the wet margin, and over the next twelve months as we establish the plants and as the insect life develops I hope we shall regularly be seeing herons and kingfisher, grey and pied wagtails, a few mallard and possibly moorhen.

We shall move some frogs' spawn and toads' spawn from the ephemeral pools on the forestry tracks nearby and we know that within two years the pond will be alive with water insects and other invertebrates as the whole chain of pond life builds up – provided of course that we keep the invading Muscovies at bay!

GARDEN PONDS

A pond is an invaluable addition to any birdwater's garden, and it can be made quite easily and cheaply. Choose a low-lying or waterlogged location if possible. Dig a hole with sloping sides and a gently shelving bottom, leaving a shallow rim on part of the perimeter for plants (and for birds to stand on while drinking or bathing; a large rock or two protruding from the surface of the water can serve a similar purpose). Line the hole with old newspapers or magazines, first soaked in water if it is a windy day so that they will not blow about. On top of these lay a large plastic sheet, weighing it down at the edge with either paving stones or grass turves.

Establish plants gradually. Among the best to choose, depending on the size of your pond, are common reed, bullrush (reedmace), yellow flag and water plantain, floating pond weed, water milfoil and water starwort. Stocking the pond with fish or tadpoles is essential if you wish to attract fish-eating birds such as kingfishers, or even herons. The latter will reduce your stock in no time at all.

SUMMER

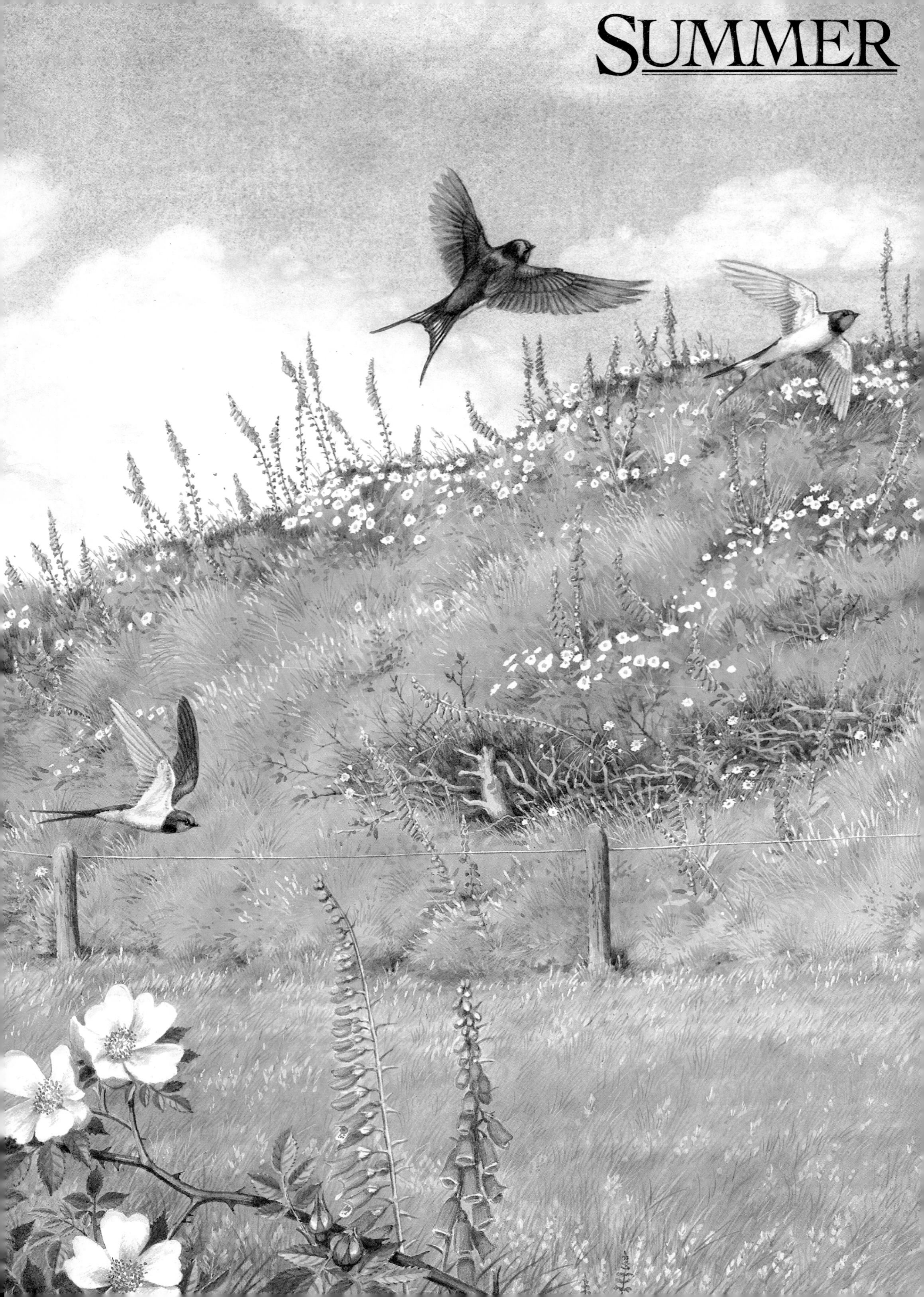

SUMMER

ummer, the climax of the birds' year, is a time of maximum productivity and food in plenty, with birds of most species at their highest numbers.

For us as neighbours and human observers of their scene it is apparently a season of fullness and easy living. As the summer months slide by, the pace of life relaxes and the frenzy of spring activity subsides throughout June and lapses into the lazy days of July and August. If there has to be an end and a beginning to the year for birds it reaches its zenith now, in summer. None the less the picture is never clear-cut, and birds continue to bemuse us with the individual complexities of their timings and patterns: the crossbills in the pine forests finished breeding four months ago, while many of our garden birds are still producing summer broods, with more still to come; woodpigeon pairs have yet to start breeding, but adult cuckoos have already left our shores. The first returning northern travellers drift back from the Arctic wastes, and seabird colonies round the coasts, pungent with the heavy odour of fishy refuse, are full of gauche and unattractive young.

Despite this confused pattern the height of summer provides birdwatchers with many of the strongest and most lasting memories of the year, images to draw on in the long months of autumn and winter. Swifts wheel, screaming, high in the fading light of summer evenings, the mellow richness of a solo blackbird can be heard in the heat of day when all else rests, and swallows skim low over the cattle pastures through the long days.

At this season of summer fecundity there are young birds everywhere, innocent trainees suddenly released into the hard ways of the real world; each must hurry to pick up the vital skills of survival if he is to be among the small minority that will overcome the hazards of their brief youth to achieve adulthood. For the young rooks in the fields below the big sycamore-tree rookery at the end of the lane the first summer will be hard-going, literally, for the baked ground will deny them access to the juicy, nourishing leather-jackets and other invertebrates on which they feed, and many of these birds will fail to survive; the mallard broods which started ten or twelve strong are already reduced to twos, threes or fours as a result of depredations by pike, gulls and other predators; and in the garden, broods of emerging blackbirds and robins are also reduced to half their size in the first few days after fledging. Fewer than half the eggs that are laid in all the nests of blackbird, song thrush, chaffinch, robin and other familiar garden birds will eventually produce flying young, though among other species which build covered nests, such as house martin, swift, blue-tit and nuthatch, the number of survivors will be a little higher.

The garden is full of squeaking young at this time – food-begging from parents, loitering ill-concealed amongst the plants in the flower border or skulking, hunched and heavy-bellied, under the hedge bottom or the flowering creepers against the wall. How many, I wonder, will live to see the plants flower again?

Song thrush feeding its young

SUMMER scene on previous pages shows a spotted flycatcher, swallows and a male blackbird.

There are already young robins from a second brood only just out of the nest. They have a penetrating, give-away food call and a gormless look heightened by the ridiculous plumes of nestling down still adhering to their crowns. Young blackbirds, too, are hopping expectantly behind their parents on the lawn and a blue-tit family, newly on the wing from a nest-box by the stream, flounders about ineptly in the apple trees.

Sadly, of the individuals which have successfully hatched and recently left the nest the majority will succumb over the next few months. Only ten to eighteen per cent of the total eggs laid in a season will result in adult birds being recruited to next year's breeding numbers. Cats and other predators hear the squeaking young robins and blackbirds as easily as we can. Tawny owls and sparrowhawks will help themselves to the harvest of inexperienced young blue-tits and other woodland birds over the following weeks. But horrific as this may sound, the alternative would be, if anything, even more alarming. Assume for a moment that one pair of blue-tits produces ten successful young and all (plus the two parents) breed again next year at the same level of success: at the end of next season the original pair would have multiplied to sixty birds and within five years – a good span for blue-tits – there would be an astronomical 15,000 birds in place of (and presumably occupying the same area as) the original pair! Sparrowhawks and other predators may vastly deplete the crop of young woodland and garden birds in June, July and August, but they not only keep us free from an overwhelming flood of smaller birds, they also help to ensure that it is the quickest, fittest, and most resourceful ones which live to breed again next year.

GRASSHOLM

For three years I tried to land on the rocky, cliffbound reserve of Grassholm island twelve miles off the Pembrokeshire coast. Here the coast is wide open to the south-west and in the eye of the prevailing wind, so any plan to land made from a distance is liable to founder. Although the cliffs of Grassholm are not high, the landing places on it are restricted to two narrow guts, one on the north side and one on the south, and a turbulent tide race between them rips past the east end of the island. Only the lightest of winds and the gentlest of seas will permit a landing and many boatloads of hopeful visitors have had to settle for a round-the-island trip instead of the intended two hours' respite on Grassholm at the end of an outward journey.

From the mainland Grassholm appears as a low hump on the horizon, but even through binoculars, at a range of twelve miles, its surface is white with a mass of gannets. It is a tiny, uninhabited island of only twenty-two acres which has been a reserve, owned by the RSPB, since the end of the Second World War. It is dominated by gannets, the largest and most magnificent of the north Atlantic seabirds. They nest on only a handful of sea-torn rocks, offshore islets and one or two mainland cliffs from Iceland down to Northern France with a few colonies on the Canadian coast. Grassholm's gannets are one of the greatest throngs in all the north Atlantic.

Our boat took over two hours to cross the lightly-moving waters and navigate the evil-looking currents, out past the other islands and through teeming flocks of different seabirds overhead and on the sea. There were herring gulls which followed us out from the land but soon left us; guillemots and razorbills resting on the surface and diving to safety in the clear green water as we approached, or taking off and flying across our bows with furiously whirring wings; manx shearwaters dark above and white below careening on the stiff narrow wings of gliding birds just above the surface of the sea. Occasionally there were little groups of puffins with their ridiculous, parrot-shaped, multi-coloured bills watching curiously as the boat swept by.

Nearer to Grassholm gannets began to predominate, in ones and twos at first, cruising overhead across our path or swinging wide on powerful thrusting wings. Then they appeared in larger parties and Indian files streaming back towards

56

An adult 'sky pointing' before flying

A second-year immature

Open-mouth threat to neighbours.

A bowing display - part of the territorial defence ritual.

Plunging into the water with closed wings.

Braking with the feet on landing.

Gannets close together on their nest mounds of seaweed and rubbish, with a well-grown downy youngster.

Razorbill

the island over which they crowded in a moving blizzard of white. Their size is impressive and the whiteness of their plumage dazzling; they are snowy-white birds with bold black wingtips, a six-foot wingspan and a bill like the end of a heavy broadsword. Against the dark sea or the blueness of the sky their whiteness is brilliant. As the little boat landed us, via a dinghy, in the narrow gut on the south side, one jump separated us from the slippery wet rocks and the much wetter certainty of clear water under the boat if one slipped. At the right moment as the dinghy rises up on the swell – not a moment before or after – we jumped one by one and all landed safely. I have landed on many islands in this way over the years and every time there is a tingling feeling of excitement and achievement as your feet land on *terra firma* leaving you to hurry up the rocks away from the splashing waves. The sky above the island was a mass of thousands of the great white birds, gliding round stiff-winged and turning their heads to look below their wings at the little knot of intruders who were moving across the rocks.

Over 20,000 pairs nest here and the atmosphere of expectation as one lands on the island and moves towards the colony is one specially reserved for those places, often remote and difficult to attain, which lead us to believe we are about to witness one of the great spectacles of the natural world.

From the top of the ridge of the island you suddenly look out over the white sea of nesting gannets which fills the western half of the island. First-time visitors do not speak when they first see the spectacle; they just stand for several minutes and take in the sight. Each incubating bird is precisely positioned, just out of stabbing range from the next. Each nest is a smooth, contoured mound, to which is added every year seaweed, grass torn up from turf on the island and flotsam of all sorts collected from the surface of the sea and decorated with the orange, blue and green of discarded netting. Excreta and mud from the space between the nests are used to plaster the materials into shape. The whole area of the colony is eight acres of suppurating gannet slum, and a mass of immaculate snow-white birds. The stench is without equal on a hot June day. The mass of birds above the island is silent, but a guttural chuckling rises and falls from the endless disputes and greetings in the colony itself.

The expanding edge of the nesting area, which is occupied by the last arrivals at the colony, is mainly populated by young pairs, some nesting for the first time, others simply holding territory and preparing for a future season. They are not as far advanced as the older and more experienced pairs either, many of whom already have grey, downy young. Around the periphery herring gulls loiter with intent, and an unguarded egg becomes a signal for a lightning incursion by the gulls.

The gannets are close and the details of their appearance clearly visible. The crown and nape of the adults have an ochrous wash at this season and the pale blue eyes, masked in black eye band, have a deeply penetrating and malevolent look. Head-on, gannets appear cross-eyed! In fact this is because of their superb bifocal vision, which is essential for

Puffins

fishing from the air. A flock of fishing gannets amongst a shoal of fish is a thrilling sight. The birds wheel and turn above the shoal then plummet down in a ceaseless rain; wings closed and massive bill extended, each hits the water with a resounding splash, disappears below the surface and comes up a second or two later having already swallowed the unfortunate prey.

Gannets fish collectively in this manner out at sea and away from the nest-site, and consequently do not have to defend a feeding territory around the nest. For this reason they can afford to nest in tight colonies and benefit from the advantages this brings by way of mutual defence (although the gannet has few enemies but Man). Colonial breeding also enhances the breeding stimulus through communal contact.

It is hard to believe the explosion of numbers that has taken place on Grassholm this century, for even within living memory there were no more than three hundred pairs (up to the time of the First World War). Now each year the colony pushes further and further across the summit ridge on to the slopes, which are catacombed with collapsed burrows once occupied by as many puffins until the whole system collapsed. The puffins had literally burrowed themselves out of existence and left. Today there are none on Grassholm and the puffin host in this corner of Wales is confined to the inshore islands of Skokholm and Skomer. Here throughout the summer months they nest in the deep turf safety of rabbit burrows on the clifftops – unlikely retreats for such colourful seabirds. They emerge from them throughout the day, somewhat improbably to gather in conversational groups and delight the visitors, for whom puffins are the number one attraction.

They feed their young on silvery sand eels which they bring to the cliffs on rapid whirring wings, running the gauntlet of marauding gulls, their bills neatly packed with the gleaming fish, sardine-like, head to tail.

Guillemots

FILMING AT MINSMERE

The BBC's Minsmere *Birdwatch* in early summer was the first of its kind. It was an exciting pioneer attempt to bring the thrills and frustrations of a day's birdwatching direct to the television screens at home, with live transmissions and recorded inserts presented at different times from dawn to dusk. There is nothing better calculated to set the adrenalin running than the prospect of taking part in live television when you cannot guarantee that your star performers will turn up. The fact that the whole day went so smoothly, with none of the crises, near-misses, blunders or confusions that could so easily result from such a highly complex operation, was an immense credit to the planning and skill of the BBC staff. Perhaps the most disconcerting aspect for the presenters – Tony Soper, Marion Foster and myself – was that we did not know whether the next bird we had to talk about was one we were actually looking at out of our respective hides or whether a 'better' picture would be offered from another camera. The result was that we had to

identify each bird by glancing surreptitiously at the monitor screens as we were talking (knowing that viewers at home were looking at an undoubtedly larger and better-quality version of this picture than the one we were trying to peep at on our tiny monitors).

The birds excelled themselves – but then, what a place Minsmere is! It is the obvious first choice for a programme of this sort, an RSPB reserve which probably offers the best opportunities for rewarding birdwatching of any single site in Britain. Throughout the preparations for televising *Birdwatch* and in the weeks building up to it there were cameras and cables seemingly everywhere and the reserve staff were marvellously helpful. On the actual day seven cameras were installed: one remote controlled, one on a high tower overlooking the whole reserve and five in hides looking over the lagoons. It was difficult to believe that any bird could arrive or depart without being on offer to us through one camera or another.

The highlights of that glorious summer day were many: the plunging osprey mobbed by a furious marsh harrier and forced to drop its catch; the grace and

Common terns
hover in buoyant flight.

The sand martins
use last year's burrows.

Graceful avocets
feeding in the shallows
at Minsmere.

elegance of the avocets around us all day and the buoyancy and delicacy of common terns and little terns on the wing. These were the jewels of a star-studded day, but I think I will remember just as long the intimate glimpses we had of the daily lives of other, less remarkable, birds that we are likely to see at any time in ordinary domestic surroundings. I particularly enjoyed the sand martins, noisy and excited as they re-excavated sandy burrows, their colony re-formed after its long sojourn south of the Sahara, and the eternal war of nerves between the quietly determined stalking herons and the black-headed gulls, forever trying to move them on by means of frenzied bombardment. I remember marvelling at the sanderlings, turnstone and dunlin, feeding earnestly, never resting: they were building energy and food reserves for the long flight still in front of them to Arctic breeding grounds. Today they were a few yards in front of us; tomorrow they would be many hundreds of miles away to the north. Minsmere at any time is a feast of birdwatching – in the early summer it can present almost more than any individual can take in.

Turnstones

A FOSTER FAMILY

In the Great Wood at Gregynog Hall the oaks are old and decaying but still huge and magnificent. Many are festooned with epiphytic (surface-growing) ferns and lichens and all have broken limbs and wind-torn branches. They stand at respectful distances from each other with no crowding so that only their outer spreading branches touch, thus filtering out most of the sunlight from the heavily grazed floor of the wood. Because these ancient trees are full of holes, crevices and recesses, and because oaks produce a greater harvest of insect food than any other British tree, the Great Wood is a haven for a wealth of bird life in spring and summer.

A cohort of jackdaws has commandeered the larger holes, leaving only an obligatory few for a couple of pairs of tawny owls, the graceful stock doves – the only hole-nesting pigeons in Britain – and a pair of kestrels which are nesting deep down in the hollow of a broken limb of a huge solitary ash. Starlings have grabbed most of the smaller holes, but I have put a lot of nest-boxes in the wood over the years with holes too small to admit the rowdy starlings and almost all of them are tenanted each year by pairs of busy blue-tits, great tits or bright pied flycatchers and redstarts. The blue-tits get first option on the boxes, unless I cover the holes in the early part of the season, simply because they are there before the pied flycatchers and redstarts arrive. There are plenty for both, however, and this year it was a surprise on one of my regular visits to find that a pair of flycatchers had been usurped by blue-tits which had taken over the nest and added their eggs to those already laid by the flycatchers. On the next visit, to my further surprise, the blue-tits had successfully hatched not only their own nine eggs but three of the flycatchers' also and

The foster family

were feeding a mixed brood of lusty youngsters!

And so it continued. The flycatchers prospered on the same diet of green caterpillars that their real parents would have brought, and eventually all twelve left the box and became a mixed family of insatiable, demanding youngsters pursuing the parent blue-tits clumsily through the oak branches around the nest-site.

Such accidental fostering does occur from time to time, usually as a result of competition for nest-sites, and is completely different from intentional parasitizing of other species' nests, for example by the cuckoo. But it can only be successful fortuitously, and if the incubation period, general behaviour and feeding of the two species are similar; even then there must be many failures.

I shall never know, of course, whether the flycatchers eventually survived to find their autumn route to the south – or whether, if they did, they then believed they were blue-tits or pied flycatchers!

SHELDUCKS

Shelducks, the largest of Britain's ducks, are the most colourful and conspicuous of our coastal birds. They live on low sandy and muddy estuaries and shorelines all round Britain and are the only one of our wildfowl species to do so.

They are large, goose-like birds which feed mainly on tiny gastropod snails called *hydrobia*, which they scoop up in numbers from the surface of exposed tidal mud and sift with their bills, or they up-end for them from the surface of the water as the tide comes in and covers the mud flats.

Shelducks are seldom seen inland. However, they can sometimes spring surprises. In early summer I was in one of the ancient relics of primeval oakwood in Suffolk, a mile or two from the coast, when I was taken completely unawares by several shelducks flying amongst the oaks ahead of me. Four or five birds rose from the ground out of the bracken and I saw two more sitting in the crown of a massive oak, before they decided I was too close and beat off through the wood and away towards the coastal marshes.

Improbable though their appearance there seemed, I recalled that these ducks will travel several miles if necessary, even away from the coast, to find suitable nest-sites. They breed in the dark recesses of old rabbit burrows, holes at the base of trees and similar – even, at times, as I had witnessed, large holes higher up in trees. Their breeding territories, and therefore the number of pairs able to occupy a given area, are determined in an interesting way. The availability of nest-sites is not the limiting factor because they are fairly adaptable and also prepared to travel, and although they are quarrelsome birds on the feeding grounds they will sometimes nest almost side by side.

From late winter the individual pairs set about establishing their exclusive feeding territories on the best areas of the muddy estuary and coast. They defend these vigorously, and once all the available space has been divided up in this way between the pairs those without an adequate feeding territory will be unable to breed that season.

Once nesting begins, in late May, the female's task is to incubate the eggs (she leaves regularly twice a day to join the male and feed) and the male's responsibility is to retain the feeding territory and defend it against all intruders. All the young hatch simultaneously and both adults then lead the tiny ducklings on their overland migration to the reserved feeding area on the coast, the female leading and the drake bringing up the rear. The downy ducklings, in harlequin patterns of black and white, are the most engaging and attractive of all our native ducks.

Here on the Suffolk coast and elsewhere round our shores pairs of shelduck now stand guard by the broods of growing youngsters, but the size of some of the 'broods' is strange, to say the least – twenty or thirty in some cases. The explanation lies in the aggressive nature of the adults, which results in frequent skirmishes with neighbours during which the broods often become muddled up and swim off happily with whichever parents come back first! The female, troublemaker that she is, is often the instigator of the boundary disputes, lowering her head and pointing with her bill to arouse the male to action. The male almost always accepts the call to duty, first with deep, jerky warning movements of the head, quickly followed by headlong pursuit of the object of the female's annoyance, which can result in considerable scuffle and commotion.

As July progresses another shelduck phenomenon is unfolded. Leaving a handful of 'nurse' adults behind to look after all the young, which are gathered together in crèches of as many as a hundred or more, the entire adult population leaves on a long flight to one special area off the German coast where virtually all the shelducks from north-western Europe congregate for their annual moult and the entailed period of flightlessness. It is no great distance across the North Sea for the Suffolk birds, but even those from as far away as the west of Ireland, the coasts of Norway and the Baltic make the strange return journey each year, and the reasons why the birds all congregate at this one place to moult (there is also a smaller moulting area in Bridgewater Bay, Somerset) remain obscure. Until the adults drift back in September and October the coastal creeks and lagoons of Suffolk – and all the other low, muddy shores and estuaries round the British coasts – will be left to the maturing groups of juveniles, now in their unpretentious patchwork plumage. The few adults that remained with them will have completed their own moult during this time and now await the return of the main body of migrants from the mud flats on the other side of the North Sea.

Shelduck feed on tiny snails
in the muddy shallows

The female,
by horizontal pointing,
induces the male
to pursue intruders.

Both parents lead
the newly-hatched brood to the shoreline.

WORKING PARTS

Identifying birds is much easier when you know the names of their main external features. The combinations of colours, shapes and sizes of the topographical features are infinite, so it is of immeasurable help to know which in particular to look for when trying to distinguish one species from another. For example, in grey geese the colours of the legs and bills are particularly important; in ducks it is a good idea to take note of the speculum, or wing patch, especially in the more difficult-to-recognize females; lengths of legs and bills are obvious features to check in waders, and it is important to look for the presence or absence of wing bars and the extent of white, if any, showing on the rump. Marsh-tits and willow-tits can be more easily identified by looking at the respective size of the chin patch and the extent of the black crown. The combination of eyestripes and wing bars help to distinguish some of the leaf warblers, while eye colour will help determine owl species.

It is good training to practise recording the details of birds you see in the garden at home (see page 18), listing the different features even of the commonest species in order to familiarize yourself with the names of each part. Also, try describing the features of a common bird – say, a blue-tit or great tit – without looking at it: you will find this a salutory lesson!

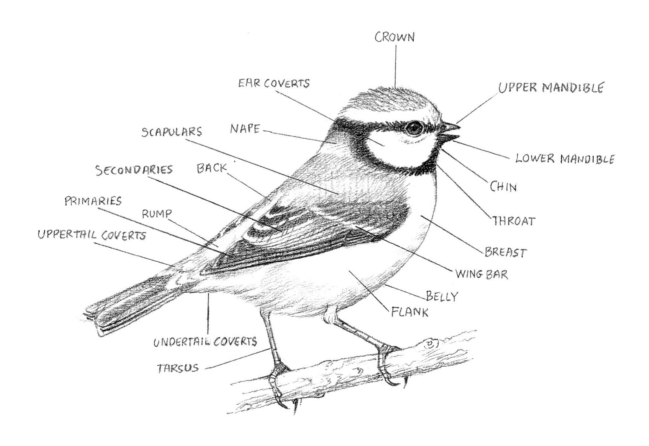

BLUE-TIT

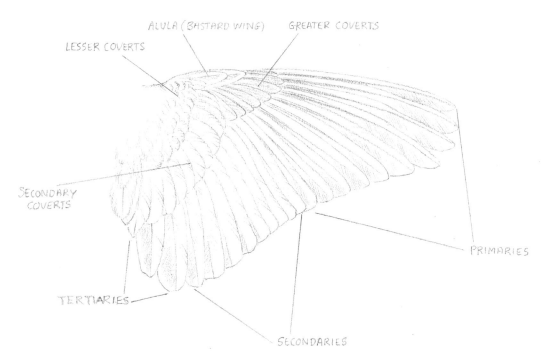

LESSER COVERTS
ALULA (BASTARD WING)
GREATER COVERTS
SECONDARY COVERTS
PRIMARIES
TERTIARIES
SECONDARIES

Each feather on a bird's wing plays its part in enabling the bird to fly. The primaries, the largest feathers, propel the bird through the air. The secondaries help to keep the bird in flight. The coverts cover the quill base of the larger feathers giving the wing an aerodynamically smooth surface. The alula feathers help to control flight.

Birds' feet are adapted to their life-style, habitat and, often, the food they eat. With three toes pointing forward, and the fourth to the rear, a bird's feet differ according to whether it is a percher, like the chaffinch; a climber, like the green woodpecker; a bird of prey, like the sparrowhawk, or a swimming bird, like the black-crested grebe.

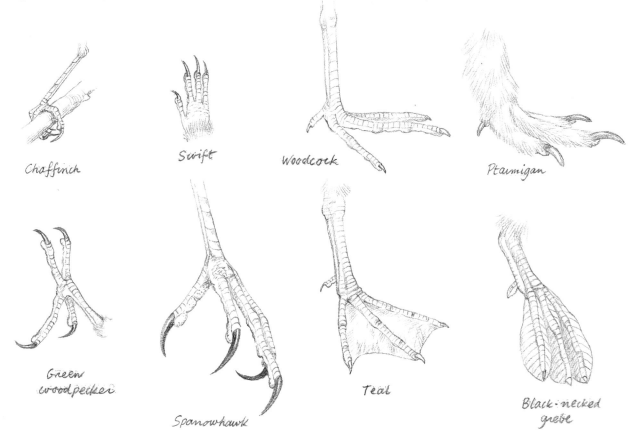

Chaffinch

Swift

Woodcock

Ptarmigan

Green woodpecker

Sparrowhawk

Teal

Black-necked grebe

BUZZARDS

This is the time of the year when each valley in western Britain rings with the incessant and monotonous call of young buzzards, now on the wing and pursuing their parents with wheezy food-begging cries, 'eeeee-ya', which rise in pitch and excitement on the approach of food. In much the same way as the repeated 'pink' alarm call of chaffinches or the incessant and feeble 'tseep' of reed buntings becomes tiresome, the food calls of young buzzards are one of nature's more irritating noises, so unlike the melancholy but evocative mewing of the adult birds.

Buzzards are able to take advantage of a wide selection of foods, far beyond the fondness for rabbits with which they are conventionally credited. Such adaptability is part of their huge success and will have an important bearing on the success of the young birds over their first weeks of independence through the summer and autumn. Buzzards are slow-moving, broad-winged hawks lacking any notable agility, therefore they have to hunt by methods which cannot rely on the speed and dash of a peregrine or sparrowhawk, or the agility of a harrier or hobby. By slow soaring on stiff wings they scan the countryside for carrion or other potential prey, but they also spend much time sitting on fence posts, telephone poles or tree branches in favoured hunting areas waiting to locate prey before gliding silently down from their lookout post to take it unawares.

All manner of small mammals are within the buzzard's compass, up to the size of rabbits and young hares, but they will also feed willingly on nestling and fledgling birds, amphibians, reptiles (I have watched a buzzard fly off trailing a writhing three-foot-long grass snake) and in fact almost any animal matter they can find. They are proficient at hovering, kestrel-like, especially in the face of a stiff breeze, but they also spend a lot of time, often in the early mornings, walking about in the dewy fields collecting earthworms and larger insects; they eat a lot of earthworms, especially at this time of year, but of course none of the remains of these shows up in the pellets of indigestible items which are regurgitated from the stomach instead of being passed right through the system.

Birds of prey are the best-known group to produce pellets, although many other species do so too. Pellets provide some valuable clues as to what the birds have been eating. Generally they are made up of the hard, indigestible wing-cases of insects, small mammal bones, fur, feathers, teeth of mammal prey, beaks and claws, and so on. Some birds – rooks, for example – produce vegetable-based pellets of grain husks or similar material. The range of birds ejecting casts in this manner is very wide; it includes unexpected species such as dipper, starling, pied wagtail, robin, some warblers, kingfisher, spotted flycatcher, members of the crow family and heron. Pellets vary greatly in size, depending on the size of the bird that produces them. Broadly speaking they are dark in colour, scentless (but musty if they are at all old) and tapered cylindrical in shape. Their origins are often almost impossible to identify unless they come from known roosting or nesting sites. Pellets can be taken apart by floating them in a shallow dish of water and separating out the hard pieces. Several guides are available to aid identification of small mammal skulls and other bones examined in this way. Some people mount the hard remains on card for future reference.

A dark buzzard feeding on worms in a field

Soaring stiff winged
on the rising air currents

Rabbits are a favourite food of buzzards

Buzzards spend long periods
sitting on trees, waiting for prey

Buzzards occasionally take grass snakes

HERONS

High summer also sees the young herons at last leaving the worsening squalor of their nests, now plastered with encrusted droppings and festooned with the dried-up remains of spillage from regurgitated meals. After the recent weeks of wing flapping and exploratory flights in the tree-tops, they are free-flying and putting their resources to the test in the real world. At about nine weeks of age they will still receive some supplementary help from the parents when they food-beg for regurgitated morsels, but very soon they will be independent. A number of them will already be wandering considerable distances from the colony at this time. This is a season of plenty, however, and they should not have too much trouble making their way in the coming weeks; the winter will be their first real test.

These young birds have none of the brightness or panache of the adult birds; they are a drab grey and white without the yellow bill, black plumes and eyestripes of their parents.

We traditionally think of herons as fish-eating birds but their diets are in fact far more catholic than this. Apart from fishing the backwaters, ponds and riversides the young herons will hunt swamps and marshes for newts and frogs, stalk the new stubble fields in search of voles, young rats, moles and field mice, and help themselves from the store of fledgling birds, fat and flightless, which abound in the waterside vegetation and betray their presence by incessant food calls. It is a time of experiment and experience for the young herons. It is also a time of potential conflict with Man, for one of their least popular habits at this time of year is succumbing to the temptations of easy pickings offered by the increasing numbers of fish farms up and down the country: here in the early hours of summer mornings, before the staff are about, the herons, often from heronries far removed from the area, gather to sharpen their hunting skills by sampling the captive stock.

A young heron

SUMMER BIRDS FROM THE NORTH

By July, the best of summer has already passed for some of the visiting birds. The cuckoos which brightened the days of May and June have already left, a week or two ago; the screaming swifts will soon be missing again from the skies above our towns and villages and even the meadow pipits and other upland birds are moving off the hills.

At the same time that we begin to notice the departure of these short-stay visitors we find some compensation in the first returning travellers from further north. It is a long haul for small wading birds like sanderling, curlew sandpiper and spotted redshank from their wintering areas in the tropics and sub-tropics to the barren Arctic breeding grounds. Moreover, for those which make this great journey to the high Arctic to breed it is a hazardous and uncertain business very much, at the mercy of the weather and the timing of the summer thaw which uncovers the ground. At best a tiny sanderling or a curlew sandpiper will have only eight weeks to

complete the whole breeding cycle and move out again with its young. At worst the thaw will be too late and the summer then too short to enable breeding to take place at all: in such cases the journey will have been futile and must now be repeated.

To help compensate for these hazards over which they have no control sanderlings and one or two other high Arctic waders have evolved the extraordinary capability of producing two broods simultaneously, although not all pairs do so nor is it a regular occurrence in all areas. The female lays one clutch which the male incubates while she makes another nest nearby and lays a second set of eggs which she incubates herself. The respective broods are then reared by each parent independently.

It is the unsuccessful breeders which are the first to reach us again in July. Having failed to raise offspring there is no point in their lingering in the north and so they begin a more leisurely journey south. In spring they have hurried northwards still in their winter plumage or with only the beginnings of their breeding dress showing: now in full splendour and awaiting

The greenshank breeds sparingly on the Scottish hills.

A spotted redshank
in summer plumage-
the most beautiful of waders

A curlew sandpiper
in brick-red summer plumage

Rusty-brown sanderlings in summer plumage,
feeding at the edge of the tide, with greenshanks beyond.

Bar-tailed godwits return to Britain early
if their breeding attempt in the north fails.

their autumn moult they give us an unusual chance to see them at their colourful best. On coastal lagoons and pools the familiar silvery form of the scurrying sanderling with jet-black wet-look legs and bill is now revealed as a beautiful rusty brown bird with pure white belly. On the same lagoons or on inland sewage farms or reservoir edges the handsome spotted redshank can be seen, jet-black and spangled with white spots; his legs are dark crimson instead of winter orange. This is the most striking of wader transformations, a far cry from the slender pale grey bird of autumn, spring and winter.

Similarly the first curlew sandpiper, a tiny wader whose decurved bill earns it the first part of its name, has brick-red underparts and black and chestnut upper parts in summer instead of the grey and white of autumn and spring: it is on its way back from a fruitless trip to northern Siberia. Other precursors of the returning tribe of northern waders include occasional greenshanks – long-legged, pale and graceful – from the moorlands of Scandinavia; green sandpipers from the forest clearings of Baltic countries now stopping off on pools, riversides and other freshwater places; and bar-tailed godwits from Lapland – tall, elegant and long-billed, dropping on to the food-rich mud of the east-coast estuaries. This summer has been unkind to them all as individuals but they will return again next year for another long journey to the short-lived summer of constant daylight and rich feeding in the lonely wilderness of the Arctic.

DOGDAYS AND SUMMER MOULT

In many respects the balmy days of high summer, dark and heavy in leaf, are the period of least interest and activity for the birdwatcher. In many ways, this is both the end and the beginning of the birds' year – a real in-between period. Their main function is to reproduce their kind, and the whole annual cycle is geared to this peak. Now, young seabirds are leaving the cliffs for the more friendly element of the sea, wildfowl are going into temporary retreat, wading birds – curlew, lapwing and others – are gathered into congregations and already moving to autumn gathering grounds. In the cities, gardens, woods and fields the familiar song birds are mainly distinguished by a sudden inconspicuousness and silence. The

morning chorus has ceased as there is no longer any need to defend the hard-won territory which was so vigorously protected through the months of spring and early summer; only a few late-breeding song thrushes and blackbirds sing desultory phrases in the early morning and even less in the heat of the day. None the less there are one or two bird sounds that I still associate with this time of year, in particular the wild, maniacal yaffling of green woodpeckers which have been relatively silent through the breeding season but now call stridently through the day in the woods. These large green birds with crimson crowns and lemon-coloured lower backs are presumably re-establishing their territories and ejecting the newly independent young.

There are a few species which continue to breed through the late summer: goldfinches nesting in the orchards and hedgerows, house martins sometimes still producing young as late as October, and yellow-hammers on commons and railway cuttings, still nesting as late as August. Town pigeons feed their fat squabs on the ledges of old warehouses and church towers, and in the urban parks woodpigeons, which will breed in almost any month of the year, croon their doleful song and wait for their two eggs to hatch on a flimsy stick nest in a tall laurel.

None the less it is a time for most adult birds to rebuild tired bodies, replace worn feathers and build up condition again, either for the long migration to come or for the rigours of distant winter. The breeding season is a heavily taxing time for parent birds. A pair of blackbirds, song thrushes, robins or wrens may have as many as three broods in a season stretching from the first establishment of a territory in March to the final independence of the last brood in late July. The physical drain on the females must be enormous: in the case of a blue-tit laying twelve or thirteen eggs at daily intervals the total weight of the clutch is equal to the weight of the female herself. Similarly a blackbird's three successive clutches are equivalent to the weight of the female. In addition, the successive broods commit the parents to an endless search for food to satisfy the growing young, a demand which itself increases as the young get bigger and their needs increase accordingly. By the end of the summer the adult birds are but poor shadows of their immaculate state four months earlier.

This time of year is therefore when worn-out feathers are replaced, by moulting then growing new ones in their place. The care of feathers, so necessary for warmth, flight, camouflage or display, is important throughout the year, and this annual renewal especially so. Most birds undergo a complete moult of flight feathers and body feathers at the end of the breeding season, although the young of many garden and woodland species limit their moult at this stage to body feathers and make do with their flight feathers. They have had these only two or three months and will keep them right through to the end of the following summer.

Moult is itself a time of stress for birds and also a time when they are more than usually vulnerable to predators and other risks. This is one reason why they are so inconspicuous in high summer, spending much of their time skulking in undergrowth and other thick cover until the few weeks of moulting are complete.

The main flight feathers (primaries) are usually moulted first, followed by the secondary flight feathers and the tail, whilst the moult of body feathers goes on throughout.

Wildfowl present a very special situation during their moult, for all ducks, geese and swans lose their flight feathers at one go and are consequently completely flightless for periods ranging from three weeks (for smaller ducks) to up to seven weeks for the larger swans. During this period of flightlessness ducks spend most of their time in disconsolate groups in reedbeds and amongst other protective cover. It is interesting to note that as part of this process the drakes temporarily lose their full adult plumage and go into the relative obscurity of a drab 'eclipse' dress in which they more closely resemble the females. Thus the mallard drake with bottle-green head, white neck

Mallards in moult

75

ring and chestnut breast appears uniformly brown for a few weeks, betrayed only his his permanently yellow bill, before re-emerging in his familiar garb.

REEDBED BIRDS

The hidden world of the reedbeds is a rich and changing scene of water, scrub, reeds and sky, a world populated by a community of specialists evolved over the ages to take advantage of the unusual opportunities offered – bittern, marsh harrier, reed warbler and bearded tit – and by many other less specialized species which also benefit from its thick cover and abundant food supply.

The vast expanses of reedbeds which once comprised the fenlands of Hereward the Wake have long since been drained and turned into high-grade agricultural land. Now only small and scattered areas remain, mostly in East Anglia but also in other corners of the country; some of these are individually large enough to retain important examples of bird communities which must once have been numerous.

Within the ever-changing world of a reedbed a number of bird species survive and prosper, a few of them being specialists that have evolved to depend almost exclusively on the strange and limited world of vertical reeds. These reeds – still prized as the raw material of the thatcher's trade – remain all winter and right through the next spring and summer as firm canes supporting a waving sea of frothy heads. Often the reeds will reach a height of eight or nine feet, especially when growing straight from open waters. They stand there, rarely flattened by winter's storms until they are supplanted by the next year's mature growth at the end of the summer. By this time they have been a source of winter food for a host of visitors and have provided nesting sites and a more permanent home for a few highly specialized birds.

No reedbed bird is more specialized than the bearded tit, which spends its whole life in the forest of reeds. It feeds in summer on larvae of wainscot moth which emerge from the stems and on the aphids and other myriad insects which inhabit the reeds; in winter it exploits the harvest of seeds in the drooping heads at the top of the tall stems. A ringing 'ping-ping' locates the birds as they move around in the reeds but they do not always reveal themselves and can be annoyingly difficult to see. They are scarce and

local birds now, mainly because so few areas are suitable for them, but in addition they suffer badly in hard winters and when heavy snow covers the heads of the reeds.

The male bearded tit has a grey head with bold black moustaches and a prominent black patch under the tail. Both sexes are tawny brown above and grey below but the female is much the drabber of the two. The nest is built in the tangle of broken reeds at the base of the reedbeds and the birds are masters of the fast descent, sliding down the reed stems with legs wide apart.

As its name suggests, the reed warbler is another specialist in this hidden world. A summer visitor, it arrives in late April and May and its low churring song from deep in the reeds soon becomes the predominant sound of the reedbeds. The nest – so often host for the uninvited cuckoos – is a masterpiece of craftsmanship, built across several stems of reed three feet or so above the water surface.

The litter of decaying stems which forms the base of the reedbeds (and gradually helps transform it into firm ground) is the province of one or two other species which are specially adapted to a reedbed life at ground-level. The rare and secretive bittern with its fog-horn booming skulks in the cover of reeds stalking frogs, water voles, fledgling birds, eels and other fish. When it flies it often makes only short excursions across the reeds to other open-water edges. A loose nest of reeds is made on the dead mat of vegetation and the brick patterning of black and brown disguises the birds perfectly when they stand motionless in the reeds, neck outstretched and bill pointing upwards.

In Britain we are poorly provided with marshland rails and crakes and the only common one is the elusive water rail. It is fairly plentiful and although secretive and difficult to see it most frequently betrays its presence by a miscellany of grunts and spine-chilling squeals. It has a somewhat sinister look about it and a murderous streak to go with it, for it will supplement its catholic diet with young birds, eggs or indeed almost anything of acceptable size; I have seen one kill and pluck an adult sedge warbler in next to no time, after the unlucky bird had got caught in fishing line at the edge of the water. Water rails are perfectly adapted for threading their way sinuously amongst the vertical canes; their bodies have a slightly compressed shape which allows them to move without difficulty through the close-set stems.

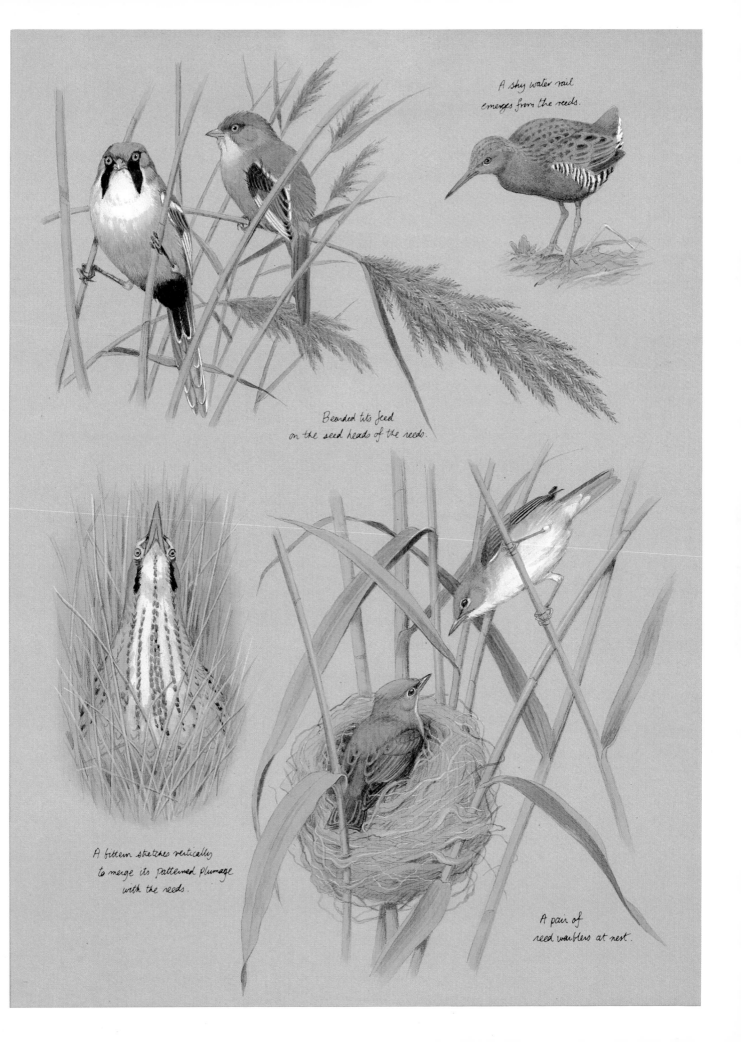

A shy water rail
emerges from the reeds.

Bearded tits feed
on the seed heads of the reeds.

A bittern stretches vertically
to merge its patterned plumage
with the reeds.

A pair of
reed warblers at nest.

Collared dove

DOVES

If one includes the feral (town) pigeon as a legitimate – albeit mongrel – wild bird in its own right, but discounts the thoroughly domesticated breeds of homers, tumblers, tipplers and rollers, we have six species of pigeons and doves in Britain, five of them resident and one, the turtle dove, a summer visitor. Woodpigeons, and even more so feral pigeons, are an ever-present part of our scene through the year but in other ways late summer is the time I especially associate with the pigeon family. Rock doves, from which stock our domesticated strains originated, are birds I have watched on many summer days on the western coasts of Scotland or Ireland. Nearer to home the crooning of woodpigeons evokes hot summer days; turtle doves, too, conjure up a vision of high summer, purring softly through the heat of the day when most other birds are silent.

The collared dove is the most recent addition to the family of pigeons. It is a somewhat nondescript bird, uniformly fawn-coloured, relieved only by a neat black half-collar, but it has a quite remarkable history. Formerly found in south-east Europe and the Middle East it expanded its range more successfully and dramatically than any other European bird in recent times. It reached our shores as recently as 1955 but within ten years it had covered the whole country and has long since become a very familiar town and country bird. Its success was so dramatic that it had the unenviable distinction of gaining a place on the official list of pest species within twenty years of its arrival.

Collared doves associate freely with Man and are particularly at home in, for example, suburban surroundings such as town parks as well as in rural areas. There, their attraction to grain stores has made them thoroughly unpopular. They have been in our garden at home for several years now and although their repetitive cooing call can become boring they bring us a lot of amusement and interest and there is still much we do not understand about them. Ours disappear in winter and go goodness-knows-where, but they are back by February if the weather is mild and they produce successive broods onwards through the year. In late summer there is great activity as they fly ceaselessly to and fro in pairs, rather like doting couples who will not go anywhere without each other. One flies from one of the big fir trees to another and the partner goes too. They sit a while, the male coos spasmodically and then they move off again, wing tip by wing tip, to the television aerial, the stable roof or the big beech tree by the bridge. So it goes on all

Turtle doves feeding

Stock doves

through the day, the pair flying together back and forth across the garden bowing and cooing at a time of year when most other birds are silent. They keep it up well into September, but then they are prolific breeders and will produce anything up to five broods in a season. It is little wonder they are a successful species!

I see the stock doves in completely different circumstances. They are reasonably common throughout the country but unlike most other pigeons they shun proximity to Man and live in the open countryside, where they are easily overlooked amongst the welter of woodpigeons. This is a pity because they are in fact very beautiful; their feathers are delicate shades of grey and blue, and they have an iridescent green patch on the sides of the neck and suffused pink on the breast together with the bright red feet of the remainder of their clan. They feed in green fields, often with woodpigeons, and there is one particular stretch of road where I can almost

invariably rely on seeing them at this time of year, particularly in the early morning. Like many other vegetarian birds, stock doves must take in grit to help grind down the food in their stomachs and they regularly come off the fields on to this section of road (directly from their roost sites, I imagine) to collect little particles of stone of the correct size from the sides of the road. In the early light of morning I see up to forty of them here at one time.

Woodpigeon with its young

BIRD ROCK

The River Dysynni ends its short steep course from the crags of Cader Idris by spilling into a wide, shallow tidal lagoon (unimaginatively called the Broadwater) half a mile before it cascades through the last straightened channel to its rocky outlet into Cardigan Bay. In every month of the year cormorants are one of the most numerous of many birds that can be found here. They are black-plumaged seabirds with white sides to the face and, in the breeding season, bold white thigh patches; with their heavy bodies and long serpentine necks, they have a distinctly primitive look about them. They swim low in the water – in fact, they will submerge their bodies when alarmed or suspicious and swim with only head and neck visible, protruding from the water like a periscope – and they fish the warm tidal waters off the river mouth and hunt for flounders and eels in the shallows of the Broadwater.

Cormorants are supreme submarine fishermen, experts of under-water pursuit, surface-diving with a looping jump or sliding sinuously under the water and pursuing fish with simultaneous thrusts of their strong legs. Although they are strong swimmers their dives last no more than half a minute or so and when successful they bring their fish to the surface before swallowing them. But they have an Achilles' heel: unlike most other water birds they spend relatively little time in the water, limiting it to that necessary for feeding, and when not fishing they are obliged to come to the shore-line reefs, the blocks of the breakwaters or the sand banks of the Broadwater, where they stand with wings half open to dry; for although they are birds of the sea their waterproofing is strangely sub-standard and they have to dry out regularly after fishing.

Well distributed round the shores of Britain, cormorants breed mainly in smallish colonies on the rocky coasts and islands of the western seaboard. They stay in the shallow waters close to land, although non-breeding birds and winter wanderers sometimes move inland to fish in rivers and lakes.

Singly, in lines, or sometimes in goose-like skeins, they fly upstream half-a-dozen miles to the cliffs of Bird Rock. Even through the winter they make the twice-daily journey to roost in safety on the broad ledges of the mighty cliff. Now, in mid-summer, forty or more insanitary nests are scattered amongst the rocks and boulders high up on the walls of the crag. This inland cormorant colony is a phenomenon – a throwback to the times when the sea stretched a long arm inland and washed the foot of Bird Rock.

Looking up from below, you can watch the black cormorants circle and soar round their ancestral home, a particularly weird and incongruous sight on days when mist or cloud swirls round the Rock. Primeval and suspiciously reptilian, their presence in the middle of this soft countryside dominated by the

Three adults, and
a young bird, fly in
a line to the winter roost.

Swimming low,
swallowing a flatfish.

Cormorants on their
messy nests
in the rocks.

Wings spread
to dry after fishing.

A youngster pushes its beak down its parent's throat for food.

gaunt crag has an eerie quality about it. Guttural groanings of the cormorant families emanate from the hidden nests and a nauseous waft of fishy waste drifts on the wind.

These are not the only tenants of the beetling cliffs: unlikely as it might seem, a flock of wild goats lives on the heights of the cliff. The robust billies, with shaggy coats and great curved horns, and the agile nannies lead their kids through the mists on to seemingly unscalable ledges. These are relicts from the descendants of the once abundant domesticated stock of earlier centuries, now outcast and confined to a few craggy hills such as this.

So Bird Rock stands, solitary, dramatic and massive, dominating the head of the wide valley, its brooding atmosphere engendered by the mists, the cormorants and the wild goats. But it has other moods, too, in the friendlier days of summer, and a host of other tenants. An army of jackdaws swings like spindrift back and forth across the face of the high cliffs, diving into a hundred hidden crevices in the rocks, their sharp conversational calls rising and falling on the eddies of the wind. Ravens nest here too, their sonorous croaking and great black outlines commanding the summit of the Rock. Amongst the incessant calls of jackdaws there is a higher and more

drawn-out call with a quality of wildness and abandon: chough! A bird peels off over the top of the Rock, calls twice loudly, closes its wings and careens downwards across the face. It opens its wings, stretching the black-fingered primaries, and flashes in towards the cliff. It lands with acrobatic confidence on a grassy ledge, calls again and immediately pick-axes at the turf with its red sickle bill, throwing out divots and gathering up the larvae of ants, moths and other small invertebrates.

Chough are glossy black buccaneers of the crow family. With curved crimson bills and similarly coloured legs they have none of the shiftiness or menace of carrion crows or ravens. They are confiding and carefree but rare nowadays, clinging to a foothold on the western cliffs of Wales, the Isle of Man and Ireland, with another handful in Western Scotland. There was a time when they were widely spread, from Kent to Cornwall: Gilbert White in 1773 recounted them breeding on Beachy Head and all cliffs on the Sussex coast. They also occurred inland then in several parts of the country and on the cliffs of Yorkshire and Cumbria. Even in Cornwall the Cornish chough – as the bird is often misleadingly called – eventually disappeared in 1968.

Innocent of the charges of freebooting and pillaging

Chough

which are laid at the door of many of the crow family, the engaging chough is an enemy to nobody and a delight to those who encounter it.

Another adult follows the first in a wild descent of the cliff and lands some yards away, and a bird of the year, unskilled and unpractised at these high-speed aerobatics, follows awkwardly and lands with a precautionary hop. He postures and stretches forward calling for food, but the sound is lost in the babble of jackdaws and the tremulous moaning of the cormorants.

Kestrels, the most numerous of all our birds of prey (except here in Wales where the buzzard reigns supreme), live on the cliff too amidst the Babel of noise and activity. They hang in the wind and hover over the quieter slopes below the cliffs in endless quest for voles and other small prey, but when they glide higher up over the crest of the hill their slender falcon shape is worth double-checking, for peregrines also hunt this area from their mountain cliffs on Cader Idris.

The kestrels nest here at the back of a broad, grassy ledge right up near the top of the cliff, well out of sight and totally inaccessible. As the male glides across the face of the cliff the female calls loudly 'kee, kee, kee' and flies out to join him. Together they rise on the updraught until they are circling above the pinnacle of the rock. They are small and delicate falcons and, unusually, the male is almost as large as the female.

Kestrels have adapted well to man-made countryside, even prospering in the inner cities and along motorways, but the successive generations of kestrels at Bird Rock will have seen little change over the centuries. The Rock provides them with the safe nest-site and the surrounding hillsides and rough pastures furnish all the needs of their food supply year in, year out.

Bird Rock is one of the natural wonders of Wales, an awesome fortress planted in the lacework of the little hay meadows of Dysynni amid water courses bright with crowfoot and loosestrife and marshy corners yellow with the waving plumes of iris.

Kestrels

THE KINGFISHER STREAM

The kingfishers use our stream all through the spring and summer. To know their shrill call is to guarantee many more contacts with them than one would by relying on eyes alone and it surprises me just how much kingfisher traffic I hear along this small brook. Unfortunately for the kingfishers, however, along our section of the stream few of the best fishing pools coincide with suitable perches. One day I decided to provide more perches, making use of child labour (willingly given) to help build a new weir with tree trunks. This would allow a kingfisher pool to build up behind it on one of the sunniest and least overgrown lengths. Success was immediate and within two days an early-morning check produced the first kingfisher on the post provided beside the new pool. And so it continued through the summer, a succession of local kingfishers enthralling those who approached the spot with care to watch the brilliantly-coloured birds fishing. The kingfishers use the pool regularly, sitting patiently, head slightly withdrawn, watching the stream below keenly for the movement of minnows, miller's thumb or stone loaches.

With a sudden splash the bird plunges and re-emerges to fly back to the perch with prey. It adjusts the small fish in its bill and is gone, a cobalt flash following each curve of the brook as it returns to the earthy bank lower down where the second brood of the year is ready to leave the slimy, smelling tunnel excavated in the soft earth of the stream bank which has been their nest.

At close range the kingfisher is not only brightly coloured, more tropical than temperate in its gaudiness, but it also has several unusual features. Its feet are close to its body and the tiny, coral-red legs are proportionately shorter than those of any other British birds except swifts and martins, but the bird's head, to accommodate the strong, dagger-shaped bill, is almost disproportionately large for the size of its body.

The kingfisher's flight is fast (although I have seen it outstripped from a standing start by house sparrows) and it certainly gives the impression of great speed as it flies away downstream. All the same it is not proof from avian predators, and on one river near home I have been shown the plucked remains of kingfishers by someone who actually saw a bird he was watching taken off its perch by a male sparrowhawk. The birds in that area seem to have developed a preference for kingfishers but I suppose it is reasonable to speculate that kingfishers, distinctively coloured and sitting in the open, may be more vulnerable to the attentions of sparrowhawks than we think.

Two males confront each other
in stiff posture,
hiding their white cheek patches.

A male offers fish to the female.

Newly-emerged young waiting to be fed.

SUMMER TERNS

Sandwich
tern

The tough bank of marram grass is the only plant
which grows well on the shifting sandy soil on the top
of the rocky reef. It is only a small reef just off the
coast, but the waving cap of marram is the home for a
large number of the remaining roseate terns in
Britain. They are beautiful, delicate birds with snowy
white bodies and pale grey wings relieved only by the
black cap and blackish bill. The sky above the colony
is alive with the comings and goings of birds and loud
with their rasping calls. Deep in the marram the
incubating birds call to their returning mates,

stretching their heads up high through the fronds of
marram.

Packed on to this favoured island are pairs of three
other tern species, all of them visitors to our coasts for
the short mid-summer season. The handsome
sandwich terns have set up their densely packed
colony of forty or fifty pairs on the more open ground
where the sand mingles with fine shingle tossed up by
the winter storms and the first wisps of marram are
already gaining a foothold. They are bigger birds,
more robust than the roseates, with a shaggy black cap
and yellow-tipped bills. Notoriously fickle, they are
here one year and gone the next; evidently some have
already suffered an early setback elsewhere this season
because they arrived here late, began nesting
immediately and are still incubating, whilst the earlier
arrivals are now tending the sandy-coloured
youngsters, already well grown and ceaselessly calling
for food.

On the bare, rocky spine of the islet are a few pairs
of Arctic terns and one or two common terns. The
Arctic terns' scrapes are the merest apologies for
nests, made of dry grasses drawn in to decorate little
hollows and depressions in the rocks amongst a scatter
of stunted plants of sea spurrey and sea mayweed. One
pair has a nest in the top of a tuft of sea pink pressed

Arctic terns

Common tern colony

hard against a shoulder of rock yellow with lichens. In this corner of the tern complex, too, chicks are out of many of the nests, crouching in crevices in the rocks and greeting the parents enthusiastically when they arrive with each cargo of silvery sand eels. Arctic tern fish close inshore behind the tideline, flying twenty feet or so above the sea and peering intently downwards. One checks in flight, hovers momentarily and plunges; another does the same twenty yards further on. The Arctic terns, greatest travellers in the whole bird world, are hunting in the way they have for many thousands of years. When their plunge is

fruitless they rise again, shake themselves to free the clinging droplets of water and move on once more.

The only one of the five British coastal terns which is absent from the small islet is the little tern. This small, agile and excitable bird does in fact breed only a few miles away, on a sandy beach carefully protected from the inadvertent but destructive competition from sun-seeking holiday-makers. The little tern is in many ways the most vulnerable of our terns, choosing to nest on fine sandy beaches or pebble strands which are favoured by human visitors at precisely the same season as the birds come to breed.

Little terns

AUTUMN

Autumn is essentially the season when everything must change, for birds as well as for the countryside at large. It is a time of mass movement, when the rich feeding areas of Britain, especially the coastal areas, are the crossroads of north-west Europe. The general picture of an exodus of Arctic and northern European breeding birds towards wintering areas in southern Europe and Africa is complicated by other, simultaneous movements, especially large-scale emigration of birds from central and eastern Europe towards the milder countries of the Atlantic seaboard.

On a local level our resident birds take advantage of the harvest of autumn to replenish tired bodies and prepare for the approaching winter.

After the period of relative anticlimax in late summer, following the vigour of the breeding season and then the enforced moult, September hastens the pace of activity. Birds everywhere are back in evidence and on the move once more.

The hypnotic and soporific heaviness of summer passes and early autumn somehow has a welcome touch of freshness to it. Even now the horse chestnuts, earliest of all trees to change colour, are bringing the first splashes of yellows and browns to town parks and country roadsides; and even if the tangle of roadside verge vegetation is looking tired and spent, great shocking-pink banks of rosebay willow herb on railway banks, woodland edges and urban wastelands, and fields scattered with the unwelcome strands of purple marsh thistles, spear thistles and yellow ragwort reinforce the colours of the countryside. Bare stubble fields and new swards of green replace the waving acres of corn and hayfields, and open up huge areas for foraging flocks of starlings, lapwings, rooks, jackdaws, gulls and finches; these now feed on the rich pickings of uncountable insect larvae and other invertebrates and spilled seeds in the soil, much of which was denied them when the uncut crops filled the fields.

Goldfinches are one species which suddenly seems to materialize from nowhere at this time of year. They have a drawn-out breeding season but except for one pair which nested high up in a cupressus last year (and which the local cats destroyed) I see little of them

AUTUMN scene on previous pages shows a fieldfare, redwings, a female blackbird and rooks.

through summer until about now. Suddenly they can be seen every day swinging on the heads of the tall marsh thistles and ragwort in the meadow and rising twittering in small colourful parties from the heads of the burdock and hardhead on the side of the lane as each motor vehicle passes by. They feed almost exclusively on weed seeds and are especially attracted at this time of year to unkempt allotments, railway sidings, fallow fields and similar areas that provide a host of seeding plants.

A few years ago I was misguided enough to encourage the irrepressible giant hogweed to establish itself around the house simply because its sheer size (at up to fifteen feet tall it is the largest of all our non-woody wild plants), its beautiful symmetry and enormous umbels of white flowers are so satisfying and attractive. However, not only can the juices from its stem produce nasty skin rashes but it is an accomplished colonizer, almost impossible to restrain, and, Triffid-like, is all-consuming; it will take over the garden in no time, and probably the house as well if given a chance. The goldfinches love it, however, and make a bee-line for it now. They have larger bills than most of their family, sharply pointed to probe into the heads of dandelion, thistle and teasel, but they need few of these refinements to probe amongst the table-top umbels of the giant hogweed, ten feet or so above the ground. Frequently the goldfinches share the plants with young, clean-cut willow warblers, which move about amongst the massive leaves foraging on the plague of greenfly and other small insects which feed on the giant plants.

At this time of year goldfinches, being somewhat late breeders, are not at their most colourful and are still completing their moult. All the same it is easy to understand why such a colourful bird should have been so popular as a cage bird (and indeed still is in many of the Mediterranean countries). In Britain it is now illegal to catch wild goldfinches, or any other song bird, except by special licence, but the numbers which used to be caught for sale as cage birds almost defied belief. On the South Downs in Sussex, which was one of the principal areas, by no means the only one, for catching various species on their autumn migration, it is claimed that over 130,000 were caught annually in the middle of the last century in the Worthing region alone. This bird trapping had a telling effect on the numbers in Britain, and although they have now built up again there is still a heavy toll

Rooks in an autumn field

in south-west France and Iberia every autumn of birds that have flown south from Britain.

Chaffinches, ubiquitous and most numerous and familiar of all our finches, are congregating at the end of their breeding season, too. Near home there is one quiet corner of the road which is flanked by two big oak trees and a thick, straggling length of hedge. One or two pairs of chaffinches breed here in the spring and the old birds use the same territory each year, defending it with vigour against neighbours of the same species; but after breeding the boundaries break down although the individuals themselves, young and old, will remain thereabouts through autumn and winter, one or two family groups of males, females and first-year birds combining.

As I pass by they fly up into the lower branches of the oaks – silently, without any call. They sit there quietly or perhaps they spend a few moments wiping their bills or adjusting individual feathers, drawing them carefully between their mandibles. Once I have moved on they drop down again one by one like falling leaves to feed on the wide mown verge on the inside of the road and on the carriageway where the trees on the other side overhang the road.

It surprises me that they are there consistently week after week through early autumn, and that there is sufficient food immediately available to sustain a dozen or more chaffinches in this one spot. I think the answer must lie in the huge numbers of tiny spangle galls which have infested the oak leaves this year. Even in advance of the fall of the first leaves the little flat galls, the size and shape of fish scales, were popping off the undersides of the leaves and pattering

down on the ground. Each tree must have supported countless thousands this year and would provide an endless supply for the chaffinches until after the final leaves had fallen and covered the ground.

From September onwards our native chaffinches are augmented by large numbers of Scandinavian birds, although these immigrants behave in notably different ways. To start with they leave their native countries in sex-separated flocks, often of enormous size, females first followed soon after by the males, and having thus separated early on they tend to remain in single-sex flocks until the return migration in spring. They do not mix much with our resident chaffinches either. The continental birds arrive via the short sea-crossing from Belgium and northern France and spread out across the country feeding on stubble fields and fallows. They work their way across the fields often in dense groups, moving like a rolling tide as the birds at the back lift up and fly to the fresh ground in front of the main body of the flock.

It is these continental birds, too, that form great gatherings on western headlands from Cornwall to North Wales preparatory to making the sea-crossing to Ireland. So it is in late September and on into October and November that I see field after field full of chaffinches – mainly females, as they move to Ireland more numerously than the males – on the headlands of Pembrokeshire or the clifftop fields on Holyhead mountain in Anglesey. Wait long enough, or be there at the right time, and they will rise high off the ground and amid much calling head off in a huge throng high over the cliffs and the sea below towards the distant coast of Ireland.

Bullfinches feed on buds in the spring
and a variety of seeds in autumn
but seldom resort to the ground to collect them.

Greenfinches feed both on the ground
and by clinging to horizontal stems.

Parties of yellowhammers glean the stubble in autumn.

The cock chaffinch –
chaffinches often feed in large autumn flocks.

The cock linnet –
linnets search waste ground and fields for autumn seeds.

Goldfinches have longer and finer bills
than other finches which enable them
to probe deep for teasel and thistle seeds.

RECOGNITION

Snipe, collared dove and puffin

Shape As birds are often seen only in silhouette, their colour and markings alone are not reliable enough for identification.

Size The tiny form of the lesser spotted woodpecker, seen here in relation to an oak leaf, confirms its identification.

Habitat The scaup always remains at sea while the almost identical tufted duck is found on fresh water.

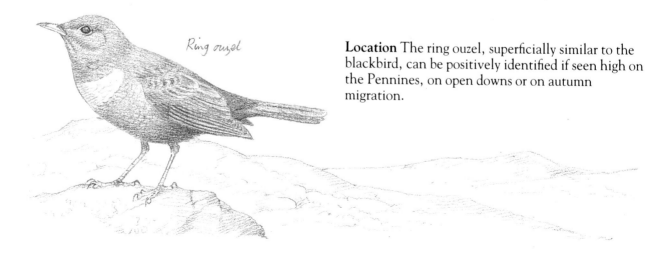

Ring ouzel

Location The ring ouzel, superficially similar to the blackbird, can be positively identified if seen high on the Pennines, on open downs or on autumn migration.

Habits The shy, undistinguished-looking dunnock tends to skulk on the ground.

Sparrowhawk and cuckoo

Flight The flight style of the fast-flying sparrowhawk confirms that it could not possibly be a cuckoo, which it otherwise resembles.

Chiffchaff and willow warbler

Song Willow warblers and chiffchaffs are hard to tell apart but their songs are totally dissimilar.

Swift - long and swept back

Peregrine - long and pointed

Rook - slotted wing tips

Wing shapes seen during flight are often a distinctive factor.

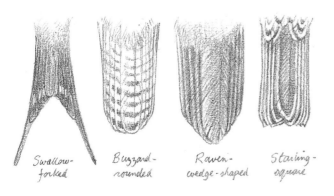

Swallow - forked

Buzzard - rounded

Raven - wedge-shaped

Starling - square

Tail shapes also show distinctive variation.

Bullfinch - white patch on rump

Goldfinch - white patch on face, bar on wings

Field marks on a bird's face, neck, rump and wings are valuable recognition guides.

GATHERING FOR MIGRATION

Once the swallows and house martins have gathered on the wires in ever-increasing numbers, autumn is truly upon us. The young swallows of the year are distinguishable by their much shorter tail streamers and paler underparts, although many of the long graceful streamers of the adult males and the slightly shorter ones of the females have become worn or broken through the season. For much of the time in the early days of these gatherings the birds sit quietly together on the wires, some leaving briefly to hawk for food while others arrive to join the company. As time goes on, however, the level and tempo of activity rise, the birds become noisier and noticeably restless; there is much preening and groups of birds leave the wires to fly round excitedly and then return again *en masse*. The time for departure is near and one morning there will be many fewer of them: the ones left behind, especially the house martins, have got late broods to complete and it may be several more weeks before the tail-enders eventually leave on their trans-equatorial journey of six thousand miles or more.

About this time other resident families are breaking up. Kingfishers may not be thought of as migrating birds, and certainly there are kingfishers on many of their regular brooks and rivers all the year round, but at the same time there is also a considerable dispersal of young birds from the successive broods of the year. I have seen this dispersal taking place on the smaller streams around home, particularly those that flow northwards out of the hills. Young kingfishers move

south up these and presumably over the watershed and into the next river catchment. I have surprised birds (and they have surprised me) well up in the hills, perhaps perched on a barbed wire fence by the narrow stream as it comes off the open hill, at other times flying along the watercourse high up the valley well beyond where I would normally expect them. All my theory and conjecture about their movement in late summer and early autumn is given some substance by the young bird I put a ring on by the brook at home one July which was picked up some months later in northern France.

Many other young birds of resident species move away from their natal areas at this time. Some are encouraged on their way by parents who now seek to keep their territories free from others of their kind in order to secure their own supply of food for the coming winter. Green woodpeckers are one example, and tawny owls and buzzards are among others which now dissuade their young from staying any longer in the vicinity.

While all this domestic sorting-out is going on the actual tide of migration can already be seen. Pied wagtails are always noticeable in our area at this time. These are insect-eating birds which thrive on insects in the smaller size-range; they are not exclusively waterside birds, as is often imagined, and although they are frequently found on sewage farms, river and reservoir banks, they are equally at home on wet pastureland, in farmyards, suburban gardens and playing fields. They are active and restless feeders, collecting most of their food from the ground and

Swallows and
house martins gathering
on telephone wires.

Pied wagtails,
adults and dun-coloured juveniles,
on autumn passage.

making flycatcher-like sallies into the air to catch flying midges and other insects. Closely mown playing fields and lawns are favoured feeding areas once their southward movement is under way, and every morning the number of pied wagtails to be counted on the school pitches and the town hall grounds gives a good indication of the pattern and strength of the movement. The black and white adults are outnumbered by the dowdy juveniles. All through September their numbers build up to a steady peak, then tail off again to leave us with just the few that will remain through the winter.

Outside the breeding season these wagtails roost communally in reedbeds and similar places where parties of birds drop in at dusk and perch for the night on the swaying stems. Many wagtails have however shown commendable initiative in developing the habit of mass roosting in the relative warmth of ledges on town buildings and even in trees in the hearts of cities, where they have a total disregard for the noise and bustle of city night-life. They have even discovered the advantages of heated greenhouses!

TIT FLOCKS

It is once more a season of variety, richness and plenty, a season which has much in store for the birdwatcher in both town and country. At this time of year noisy, bustling parties of tits may be seen on almost any walk one takes; the long-since disused railway line near here gives the best of several worlds. A sanctuary in its own right, it is also flanked by long stretches of woodland on one side and the River Severn on the other. It is one of the local places which supports wandering parties of tits at this time of year, either working along the edge of the woodland, foraging in the goat willows and young birches which

now colonize the old railway bank, or exploring the old alders, oaks and sycamores on the river bank.

These loose roving flocks are composed largely of juvenile birds, usually with blue-tits and great tits predominating, and although they give the impression of wandering freely there is actually a distinct pattern of daily movement within a fixed area. It has been shown that many of the individuals in these flocks that survive to the following spring will breed within or fairly close to the area over which the flock wandered so apparently aimlessly in the winter. As the parties of blue-, great, marsh- and coal-tits move by, the younger birds are distinguishable by their smudgier yellower appearance, lacking the white cheeks of the adults. The parties are noisy, constantly calling to each other. These contact calls play an important part in maintaining the unity of the loosely formed flock. As they pass along the railway track on their daily travels it may well be that the individual composition of the flock changes en route, affecting the adult birds in particular. Adults of several tit species, particularly marsh-tits, retain a degree of attachment to their breeding areas and are probably drawn as if by magnetism into the flock as it passes by, only to leave it again as it moves too far away from their home area. Other species too often keep

Long-tailed tit

Coal tits
and blue tit

company with the hyperactive, acrobatic tits: tree creepers and goldcrests are perhaps the most frequent travelling companions, though I have sometimes watched nuthatches and occasionally siskins travelling with them.

Foraging in flocks in this way probably has the double advantage of maximizing the birds' chances of finding good food sources and providing increased protection from predators, in so far as many eyes are clearly safer than one single pair. Through the spring and summer all the tits have fed richly on insect food but now they have to change to a vegetarian diet of seeds, nuts and fruits. In those years which produce a good crop, beechmast is particularly important and forms a crucial part of the diet for the four tit species in question. The great tit has to rely on collecting mast that has fallen on to the ground under the trees, but the smaller and more agile tits swing on the twigs in these early weeks of autumn in order to open up the seeds before they fall; however, they do need insects as well.

In towns and surburban gardens these resourceful birds turn their attention to an even wider spectrum of foods, not only profiting from the almost universal domestic provision of food but also availing themselves of other opportunities. For example, they discovered comparatively recently (around 1930, according to records) that cream in milk bottles is accessible provided a quick demolition job is first carried out on the foil tops.

The only common species of tit which does not join in the winter foraging parties is the long-tailed tit, which is exclusively insectivorous throughout the year. Outside the breeding season, family parties – or sometimes an aggregation of families – stay together and hunt through tall hedgerows and the tangle of shrubs and trees at the woodland edge.

They are easy to count as they cross a gap in the hedge or the opening of a gateway for they fly characteristically, one after another in a loose chain, contact-calling 'tsirrup' in a conversational manner, and are one of the daintiest and most delicate of all our small birds. Their plumage is pink, black and white with a bright red orbital ring, visible when seen close up, and they have very distinctive long tails which they use for balance in their acrobatic feeding.

MUTE SWANS

The brood of cygnets on the river is now reduced from the original five to three: these losses in the weeks after hatching are almost inevitable. The family is still together and the young are already much the same size as the parents although in their dull grey 'ugly-duckling' plumage they have another year to wait – sometimes longer – before they attain the full dazzling whiteness of the adults. Partly because of their great size (they are the largest of all British birds) and their pure white plumage they are among the best known of our native birds. Despite this familiarity and the special place that mute swans occupy in our affections, legends and history, and not forgetting that extra protection afforded to them as royal birds, they are subjected to widespread abuse by humans in many areas.

Many of their problems are the result of our untidiness and thoughtlessness. The debris left by fishermen, especially lead shot and discarded fishing line, cause untold problems for swans – as they do for other waterside birds. Lead poisoning from shot has contributed to the severe decline of swans on rivers such as the Thames, Trent and Stratford Avon, and discarded lines can become fatal traps for these birds. Other factors – overhead cables, river pollution,

oiling, and the inexcusable vandalism of nests and adult birds in urban areas – also contribute to the difficult lives mute swans lead in various parts of the country.

These great, elegant birds are vegetarians, sometimes grazing on the open field but more often up-ending to pull at the stems and rhizomes of water plants, using their long necks to reach up to a yard below the water surface. Both the male and the female share in building the large platform nest in spring, the male bringing supplies of reed-stems, rushes, floating vegetation and roots of water plants which the female places in position. Once the eggs are laid and the female is incubating the cob is fearless in his defence of the nest, putting on an impressive display of pent-up fury and latent power. With head drawn back, neck thickened by fluffing the feathers and wings half raised, the hissing cob is a daunting prospect. Many innocent boaters, unwittingly trespassing too close to a nest, have been put to flight by the thrusting approach of an enraged male swan.

Foxes are the main natural enemy of nesting swans, which respond by choosing a site in the watery safety of swamps, islands and reedbeds – often tantalizingly, but wisely, just beyond reach of both the foxes and small boys.

The female (pen) incubates
on a big nest of soft vegetation.

The aggressive display of the Cob
is convincing and threatening.

Three grey cygnets accompany the adult mute swans

Magpie and crow.

ROADWAY BIRDS

Roads and their verges occupy such large areas of our land surface, as well as providing a very particular type of habitat, that they obviously cannot be ignored by wildlife. In the more built-up areas the wide verges of motorways and trunk roads can take on a very special importance. Roads are both barriers to the movement of some terrestrial creatures and deathtraps for animals, birds, amphibians and insects of many sorts; for some species of scavengers, this death toll makes the highways even more interesting.

Our road system has developed its own community of avian users, albeit this community may have slightly different constituents from one part of the country to the next. In urban areas feral pigeons, street sparrows and the ubiquitous starlings make a good living from the gutters, pavements and spilled scraps on the roadway itself. I would swear that my car

passed right over a male sparrow in slow-moving traffic in London only this month, demonstrating the degree of refinement to which some of these feathered urban dwellers have got things taped. Only a little more surprising is the frequency and boldness with which blackbirds and chaffinches will tolerate human and vehicular proximity on the sides of suburban roads.

Rooks have become adept motorway feeders. They often forage on the edges of the roadway only a matter of yards from the fast-moving traffic, and are one of the principal daytime scavengers on the corpses of other birds and animals killed on roads. Carrion crows and magpies are the other diurnal operators who make the biggest contributions to cleaning up the carnage of rabbit, cat, hedgehog and other bodies killed, mainly at night. In this respect they fulfil a useful function, of course, and it is some testament to their skill that they are so infrequently victims of road

accidents themselves – even at this time of year when all youngsters, including their own, are running the gauntlet of moving traffic. It is certainly the worst time of year for wildlife fatalities on our roads, and the total number of wildlife casualties per year throughout the whole country must be astronomical. Although several local studies on the subject have been done no comprehensive survey has yet been carried out.

Pied wagtails are for me the past masters of escapology on the roads. There are many pairs with roadside territories which spend large parts of the day dodging traffic, having perfected the knack of knowing exactly when to move. I cannot remember when I last saw one dead on the road.

Moorhens seem to me to stretch their luck as jay walkers, but I have seen them on several occasions in recent years, just like the rooks, close to lanes of busy traffic.

There are various others, from the stock doves and other vegetarians which visit the roads for gritting to the tawny owls and barn owls which are so often victims at a time, I would guess, when some of them at least are benefiting from the carcasses of others on the road at night. Perhaps the saddest victim I have seen recently was a newly fledged nightjar – now so scarce – which was hawking moths at night in the light of streetlamps in a North Wales village and was fatally injured by a passing car.

BARN OWLS

It was one of those narrow lanes so characteristic of the West Country, with high banks topped by neat hedgerows and interspersed with big oaks and ashes, the twisted roots of which often stand exposed in the steep bank of the lane. Quite suddenly a barn owl appeared as I rounded one of the innumerable corners. It flew unhurriedly ahead of the car below the level of the banks and as the lane broadened and the high bank gave way to a rough, wide verge on one edge the owl was side by side with the car, no more than five yards away.

The mysticism and folklore associated with owls in general are never easier to appreciate than when the chance is given to look closely at a barn owl. There is something about their very make-up which endows them with a dimension not given to other birds. It is almost an unreality, a feeling that they belong to a different element. The mystery of owls is of course enhanced by the fact that they live a life with which we normally have little contact, dependent on the darkness, but this bird was abroad in the full light of day, strangely out of the element with which we normally associate owls.

This white and ghostly barn owl was unconcerned by the accompanying car and hunted slowly along the verge with a light and buoyant flight: the moderate size of a barn owl as gauged by its feathered outline belies the tiny frame within, concealed by the deep mass of soft feathers. Its flight is totally noiseless, thanks to the fine filaments on the tips of its flight and contour feathers, lest any sound from its wings in flight should detract from the delicacy and acuteness of hearing on which it relies for its hunting.

As it kept pace this silent white hunter turned its huge white head and looked unconcernedly at the car several times. Twice it checked in flight as if to drop into the grass and finally, after three hundred yards or

Chaffinch

When threatened, the adult flattens itself
on the ground and spreads its wings.

Long-eared owl
drawn up into
a stiff,
anxious posture.

Barn owls are great
farmyard rodent catchers.

Short-eared owls-
ground nesting birds found
on moorland and dunes.

A tawny owl gliding silently with spread wings.

The little owl,
our smallest owl,
often perches on fence posts
in daytime.

Tawny owl nesting
in a tree hole, with
two downy young.

more of travelling close to the car, it swung up over the crest of the bank and disappeared over the fields.

These owls are primarily birds of the crepuscule, the time between day and night when their spectral form seems starkly bright as they hunt over railway banks, rough marshland and field edges. Barn owls will hunt by day, too, especially when they have young to feed or when food is short towards the end of winter before the voles and mice build up their numbers again.

I watched another recently in the early morning as it hunted the rough ground in a churchyard and quartered the unkempt grass on the village common. As I arrived it swung up and settled on the top of a telegraph pole on the edge of the unfenced road. It fluffed its feathers a little then turned and looked at me; its black eyes showed boldly within its white, mask-like face – its own built-in parabolic reflector gathering the minute sounds from the ground over which it hunts and directing them to its hidden ear-openings. It gave a good view, too, of the thin, hooked bill which always seems too lightly built and delicate for the job it has to do.

After half a minute it dropped off again and several times beat up and down the common, silent but fast, fifteen feet or so above the rough grass. Once it turned and dropped solidly into the grass, feet first and head pulled back at the last minute, and vanished from view. Whatever it had pounced at was missed, however, and after a few seconds it was on the wing again, sailing over a succession of front gardens and finally settling on the wooden field gate leading out to the marshes. It shook, stretched, voided, shook again and then stood, with its characteristic hunched stance, looking all around it several times and turning its head right round to look behind it. Eventually it flew out across the marsh and was lost from view.

Over much of Britain barn owls have sadly declined in recent memory, mainly owing to the intensification of farming in the lowlands and the use of toxic chemicals, and to the removal of the old buildings and hollow trees in which they nest. At the same time, increasing numbers of farmers and landowners are responding to the encouragement of convervationists and have begun to provide artificial nest-sites in, for example, new farm buildings.

Barn owl with its prey

106

Kittiwake

SEAWATCHING

To watch seabirds I sometimes go to a particular headland on the west coast of Wales, pounded by the grey, rolling waters of the Irish Sea which break and foam at the base of the cliffs below. The gentleness of summer has gone, and the air has a chill to it as the south-west wind swirls up the cliff-face and rushes through the grasses and scrub on the clifftop.

Autumn here is a period of movement and activity as birds from the huge seabird colonies round our coasts move away towards their winter quarters. The most intrepid birdwatchers can be seen at this time braving the elements for a good view of the seabird traffic. But this is not a pastime for the faint-hearted or those of weak constitution. Clad in hat, gloves and

Manx shearwater

layers of woollies and windproofs, sustained by flasks of hot tea, you must be prepared to spend several hours in the recesses of the cliff face ignoring the cold and discomfort if you want to reap real rewards. You need a telescope, too, to pick out birds at a range of a mile or more, but your fingers will be numb from holding it after the first half-hour, even if you rest it on your knee.

There will be no shortage of inshore birds to watch – herring gulls drifting in front of the cliffs, cormorants circling the headland low over the breakers, and one or two fulmar petrels gliding stiff-winged in the updraughts.

However, once your eyes have adjusted to the distances visible through the telescope and to the ceaseless rolling of the water's surface, there will be other birds visible farther out to sea – a gannet, perhaps a mile or more distant, glistening white as it

swings to the side and gliding on long wings; behind it, still farther away, is another, and in the course of an hour over twenty passing individuals indicating the steady passage of birds. Guillemots and razorbills, too, will be visible from time to time against the distant rollers then disappearing from sight in the troughs. They fly with uneconomical whirring wings in lines of four or five, or sometimes more, and are particularly difficult to pick out against the darkness of the sea. A steady movement of gulls is taking place, too, with individuals and small groups dipping and rising above the sea as they too move towards the open Atlantic. They are kittiwakes, the most marine of our gulls, perfectly at ease far from the coasts for most of the year.

These are birds which visit our cliffs and offshore islands mainly to breed, for they resort to land only when they have a reason for doing so. The sea is their real home.

And so it continues as the hours pass. Manx shearwaters, dark above and pale below, appear and disappear close to the distant horizon, ceaselessly gliding on long, narrow wings, their wing-tips skimming the surface. Occasionally an Arctic skua or a great skua may come into view, or a passing fulmar. All are masters of the marine environment and instructive to watch in this, their true element.

Arctic skua

LINDISFARNE

Lindisfarne, or Holy Island, is famous for its early associations with Christianity; St Aidan founded a church there as long ago as AD 634. It is also an internationally important site for the huge numbers of birds, principally wildfowl and waders, which resort to it in winter. For birdwatchers Lindisfarne has a very special attraction in autumn, when the mass of arriving winter birds is supplemented by thousands more on passage.

The island lies only a few hundred yards off the coast of Northumbria, about fifteen miles south of the Scottish border, but its two hundred inhabitants are linked to the mainland by a narrow causeway which is open only at low tide and is otherwise submerged below a fierce tide race. The narrow island, less than half a mile across, extends one and a half miles from north to south and covers thirteen hundred acres, but as the tides ebb out vast areas of mud flats and sands are exposed to north and south of the island and

between it and the mainland. This fertile inter-tidal mud teems with life, with organisms which can thrive in the harsh conditions of twice-daily submergence and exposure, and it is this vast reserve of potential food which is the magnet for so many birds.

Each autumn the visiting hordes make their pilgrimage from the north and east, great squadrons of birds that prosper and breed in the short days of the Arctic summer and then retreat again before winter tightens its grip. Holy Island is a sanctuary for these travellers from the north, for there they can find the food they need through the hard months of winter.

For human visitors Lindisfarne can be bitter and raw when the north-east wind scythes across sea-birds, on the other hand, are fairly indifferent to the cold so long as they have access to their food. When I was there in autumn, however, there were many quiet days of warmth and mellowness, and it was pleasant to wander round the island's tranquil landscape.

Eider duck live here (incidentally, their down is not harvested in Britain as it is in Iceland); they breed

Eider duck feeding in the shoals

Curlew and bar-tailed godwits

numerously on the Farne Islands a little further out to sea then take up residence among the rocky shoals and reefs round Lindisfarne, diving for mussels and other bottom-living shellfish in the heaving swell. They are bulky sea duck with heavy, wedge-shaped bills and receding foreheads which give them an unmistakable outline. The drakes are boldly coloured: black and white with beautiful lime-green markings on the back of the head, although in autumn many of them are in the in-between stages of eclipse plumage, which affords them better camouflage at a time when their flight power is removed by moulting. The females are duller, brown birds. One old female I watched come in on the tide had obviously learned a particularly profitable trick. As isolated clumps of spartina grass became covered by the tide, she would dive time after time to extract the shore crabs which

had evidently been hiding in the clumps at low tide. She brought each one to the surface and, holding it by each leg in turn, shook it vigorously to break off the limbs. She would then catch the crab in the water again as it fell and finally swallow its legless body.

Out on the vastness of the flats wildfowl graze on the beds of thread-like eelgrass. Brent geese come in late October from the barren wastes of Spitzbergen and Franz Josef Land, whooper swans from Iceland, Russia and central Siberia, and thousands of wigeon share the beds of eel grass which every tide uncovers. As the tides ebb and flow they up-end to continue grazing the waving strands of grass until the depth of water is too great; then they fly off to favoured bays to wait out the tide.

As each tide creeps up over the muddy flat it pushes before it the wheeling masses of waders whose daily

Wigeon

life is locked into the cycle of the tides. As the tide ebbs they follow its edge to glean the harvest of invertebrates which seek to bury themselves in the soft mud as the water recedes; as it flows in again they retreat with it and as it floods they fly to the higher banks and the nearby fields to roost and wait for it to turn. Bar-tailed godwits are here in hundreds, probing the mud with long, sensitive bills for lugworm and ragworms; there are curlew, too, with great curved bills, prospecting for the same small creatures. Also much in evidence are grey plover, more solitary feeders who disdain the company of others of their kind; they do not probe but move in brief runs picking up the small *hydrobia* snails, shrimps and sand hoppers and pulling out the wholesome lugworms when possible. I watched one as it ran, stopped and ran again; it tilted its head to one side and fixed its eye on some slight movement across the mud, and then,

without taking its eye off it for one moment, it set off on a remarkable sideways run for fully twelve yards before it swooped on the morsel and stretched upright.

Dunlin are the most numerous waders on the flats around Lindisfarne, their numbers rising to about 14,000 in mid-winter. They are the smallest of the common shore waders and can be seen in great profusion on many of our estuaries in winter. They feed in dense packs, scurrying non-stop on the tideline, busily probing and running in constant motion.

Lindisfarne is a well-known landfall point for many other birds. Land birds, winging high above the sea and sweeping downwards into the dunes or sometimes weary and clipping low across the waves, welcome the cold elbow of land that nudges out to meet them. They will rest, feed, recover and move onward down

Redshanks and merlin at Lindisfarne

the coast. The first two days I wandered round the island there were relatively few birds on the fields or in the straggling hawthorn hedges. Suddenly, on the third day, the same fields and hedges were teeming with birds – foraging flocks of starling newly arrived from Europe, parties of redwings resting in the tall hawthorns, and solitary blackbirds in all the gardens round the village and flying ahead of me every few yards along the sheltered lanes. On the same day, too, I saw a great nervous flock of linnets and greenfinches with a few yellowhammers and chaffinches amongst them feeding on the fallen seeds in one of the cultivated fields at the end of the village.

Below the famous castle on Beblow Crag, and within a stone's throw of the sheltered harbour, there is a shallow lagoon in one of the fields – one of only two open freshwaters on the island and a natural focus for many birds. There were travel-weary lapwings in the field and a handful of golden plover with them, inland replacements for the equally dumpy grey plovers out on the mud. Noisy resident redshanks gave warning as a little cock merlin, smallest of our birds of prey, flew low along the fence at the far end of the field and then swept up to sit on the top of a skimpy hawthorn; a kestrel, which had been sitting unseen on a nearby bush, clearly resented the potential competition, took off and made a determined pass at the merlin, which ducked and then took off itself. They sparred their way bad-temperedly across the fields, twisting and turning with the breathtaking agility characteristic of their kind, and scattering all the lapwings, plover and starlings from the field. Only a pair of mute swans remained, unmoved, raising their heads to watch the commotion for a while before resuming their own preoccupations.

JAYS

Autumn is the time of plenty, with some of the easiest feeding for most species of any time of year; but the most difficult time is only just round the corner, so several species exploit the autumn feast of food by storing it for recovery during the winter. Marsh-, coal- and blue-tits will indulge in this habit, hiding berries, beechmast and other items that happen to be particularly plentiful. Nuthatches, too, will secrete hazel nuts – if the grey squirrels leave enough for them – and sometimes acorns. Rooks and woodpigeons are enthusiastic acorn-eaters and rooks can be seen visiting the oakwoods at this time of year, sometimes not waiting for the fruit to fall but pulling it from the branches while it is still *in situ*. Often they carry the acorns away and bury them in fields where they regularly probe for future use.

Without question, however, the great acorn bird is the jay. It is no coincidence that the bird's range coincides with the range of appropriate species of oaks, and the jay is heavily dependent on acorns for much of the year. At the same time, the oaks are just as dependent on the jays, for they are far and away the most important agents for the dispersal of these fruits. The heavy acorns have only one way of achieving this dispersal: they must rely on being picked up, carried away and physically planted. This the jay does with enormous efficiency.

As the acorn-gathering reaches its peak in mid-October the colourful and normally shy jay is as conspicuous as at any time of year. In the steep, wooded valleys of mid-Wales the white rump flash repeatedly catches the eye as birds move back and forth collecting the acorns in the hanging oakwood on one side of the valley and taking them across the other side to bury. Heavy-throated and often with an acorn in the bill as well they make journey after journey deftly hiding (and thus effectively planting) the acorns in soft ground, under bracken litter or in the base of bramble patches. It has been calculated that jays in any one locality can be responsible for moving well over 100,000 in a season. In this way the oaks are continually given the opportunity of spreading and recolonizing while the jays lay up stores for the winter. How efficiently they recover the acorns later in the year is open to conjecture, though it does seem that the jays retrieve many of the stores very effectively, even through a snow cover. Inevitably, however, enough are left in the ground to ensure a crop of pioneer seedlings next year.

Such is the jay's inter-relationship with acorns – the bird even has a specially widened throat to accommodate the large fruits – that it even harvests acorns which have started sprouting in the ground during the summer after dispersal, recognizing the newly growing shoots and pulling them out of the ground to feed their developing youngsters.

The 'threat display' of the jay –
raised crest and
fluffed feathers.

Alarm – the bird bobs up
and down while
calling harshly.

Great numbers of acorns are
carried away and buried
in the autumn.

The jay is the
most colourful of
the crow family.

NIGHT MIGRATION

Late at night in the suburbs of a northern town, above the sound of soft footfalls on the fallen leaves, a single thin call – 'seeep' – can be heard overhead. A few seconds later there is another call and later on another. A hundred miles away to both north and south the same thin sound falls easily on the ear in the lingering mildness of a still, autumn night. The 'seeep' calls are the sounds of redwings migrating westwards with other Scandinavian thrushes over the country. If only our eyes could penetrate the darkness as well as our ears can we should see party after party of birds moving steadfastly across the sky. After a calm, welcoming night such as this, with only light winds, morning on the east coast of England and Scotland will reveal copses and bushes full of resting and feeding blackbirds, thrushes, warblers and flycatchers where few were present the evening before.

Many birds migrate by day but just as many make their journeys at night, unseen by Man. Clues such as the early-morning arrivals and the calling of birds overhead at night suggest the presence of this invisible traffic. We are still a long way from fully comprehending the mysteries of birds' remarkable powers of navigation, infallible even in the darkness of night. Certainly the stars and the moon are their principal guides, as planetarium experiments have shown, and all the migrating species possess amazingly refined senses of orientation and distance.

The question of why some birds should choose to migrate at night is complex. They are of course safer from birds of prey at this time but that must be a relatively minor factor. A better clue lies in the fact that many of the night migrants have high metabolic rates and relatively poor heat regulation, which means that they must feed often and efficiently; as they are birds which can find their food only by day, their options are few and they are effectively compelled to migrate at night at a time of the year when the daylight hours are not long enough to accommodate both feeding and migrating.

On the other hand, birds such as swallows, swifts and martins can readily find their aerial food whilst moving: they therefore migrate by day. Birds of prey too move by day, relying on the rising air of warm thermals to give them the height necessary for long, planing glides.

After feeding during the day many of the nocturnal migrants, for example willow warblers, chiffchaffs and spotted flycatchers, become quiet as dusk approaches. Later their restlessness converts itself to movement; the peak of activity occurs from ten o'clock onwards.

Weather is the worst hazard for most migrating birds, especially in the unpredictable and changeable latitudes of temperate northern Europe. Facing a sea crossing or similarly arduous stretch, birds will instinctively wait for favourable weather, but once under way a change of wind or the onset of heavy rain can bring severe problems and may prove fatal to many. Fog is another enemy, causing the birds to lose their visual navigation markers and either grounding them – often with resulting losses – or disorientating them badly. On such nights large numbers of birds may be attracted to the beams of lighthouses, some of which have acquired unenviable reputations, despite efforts to overcome the problems, for causing large-scale bird deaths as the birds, blinded by the powerful beams, strike the light. Bardsey Island off the Llêyn peninsula in north Wales is one of these and various attempts have been made, for example by illuminating the lighthouse tower itself, to prevent such disasters.

It is hardly surprising that several of these offshore and coastal locations, which are notable as focal points for migrating birds, gave rise to a network of bird observatories after the Second World War at a time when interest in bird migration was at a peak. From Fair Isle in the Shetlands to Bardsey and Skokholm Island (now closed) off the Welsh coast, and the headlands of Gibraltar Point, Dungeness and Portland in England, established observatories have enabled ornithologists to plot, monitor and record over the years the seasonal movements of birds over Britain.

The most important technique in researching the movements of migrating birds is ringing. During the spring and autumn migrations many thousands of birds have a small metal leg ring fitted at these observatories (and many more by individual ringers throughout the country). All ringing is organized, and tightly controlled, through the British Trust for Ornithology; each ringer is thoroughly trained before being granted his government licence to trap and ring wild birds.

Nowadays the principal method of catching birds for ringing is the mist net: a fine, almost invisible net which is strung between vertical poles placed among trees or bushes. The birds fly into the net and hang in its loose folds quietly until, soon after, they are removed for ringing, none the worse for the experience. The size of rings ranges from very small ones for tiny birds such as the goldcrest or long-tailed tit to those designed for the largest of our birds, the mute swan. Special pliers are used to close the rings so that they sit evenly and comfortably on the leg. Each ring carries its own serial number and the address of the British Museum so that when it is later recovered

and returned, whether from the same locality, from some far-distant point or from overseas, it will help to build up the picture of each species' movements.

Once a bird carries one of the small metal rings it is of course individually identified for life; apart from knowledge of its movements, other important data relating to site fidelity and longevity are also gleaned from the monitoring operation. Without the ringing of individual wild birds, who would have imagined that a curlew might live to 31 years, a starling to 20 years or a swallow to 15 years?

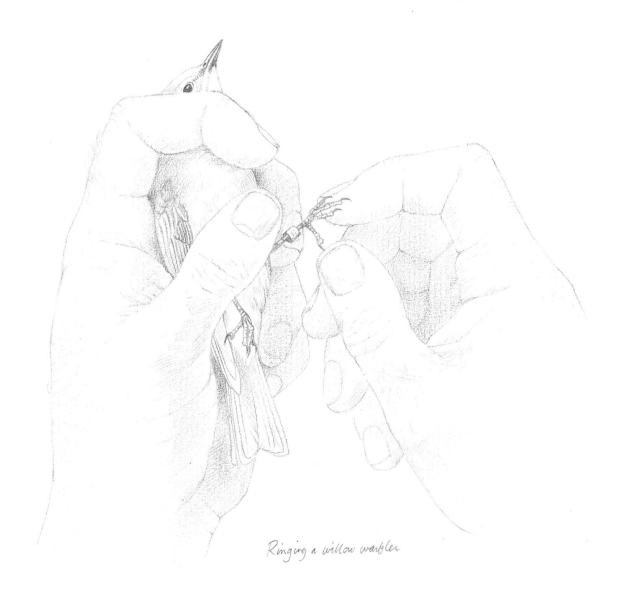

Ringing a willow warbler

Green woodpecker

WOODPECKERS

Our three species of woodpeckers dovetail with each other comfortably without overlap in the various different niches which our woodlands provide for them. By late autumn they are mostly silent and despite their bright colours they are as inconspicuous as at any time of year.

The green woodpecker, a bright mix of leaf green and lemon yellow with a crimson crown and bold, moustacial stripes, is not infrequently misidentified as an exotic rarity by unwary garden birdwatchers. They can be forgiven this mistake, for it is easy to be taken unawares by the combination of bright colours and the unexpected terrestrial habits of green woodpeckers. Although they still resort to mature woodlands to breed, boring a deep nesting chamber in the solid timber with their immensely strong and heavy bills, they are far less restricted to woods than the other two woodpeckers. Something seems to have gone mildly awry during the course of their evolution, which has resulted in their finding much of their food on the ground. They have a considerable dependence on ants and spend much time in rough pastures and parklands excavating ant hills. This makes for an easy life in spring, summer and autumn but it leaves them vulnerable when snow covers the ground in winter, when many die.

A soft 'chic' amongst the trees often betrays the whereabouts of a great spotted woodpecker as it

progresses up a tree-trunk in fast staccato hops. Its bold black and white pattern is relieved by a crimson patch under the tail, and the male also has a crimson patch on the nape. Great spotted woodpeckers obtain their food by the hard but dependable method of chiselling into dead standing timber for insect larvae, woodlice and other small invertebrates under the loose bark or deep within the timber. They need special adaptations for such work and are equipped with strong, sharp claws and stiff, thickened tail feathers which allow the tail to be used as an extra prop as the bird grips the vertical trunks and pivots to strike repeated hammer blows. To absorb such impact the skull is specially thick-walled and an amazingly long tongue probes the chisel holes to extract the wood-boring grubs that lie within.

The tiny lesser spotted woodpecker, least known but not uncommon, avoids overlap with its larger relative by using its small size and weight on the finer twigs and branches of mature trees. This means it habitually feeds higher up than the great spotted woodpecker; its small size, relative silence during much of the year and somewhat secretive habits frequently make it a difficult bird to find.

Great spotted woodpecker

The tiny lesser-spotted woodpecker is colourful but often surprisingly inconspicuous.

Male great spotted woodpecker, strong-clawed and stiff-tailed.

Juvenile.

Green woodpeckers have adapted to ground feeding - especially ants.

BIRD-TABLES

A bird-table regularly supplied with food is probably the best way to attract many varieties of birds to your garden. During a hard winter a constant supply of food on the bird-table can mean the difference between survival and death for some birds. Towards the end of autumn is a good time for putting up a bird-table, for it will give the birds time to familiarize themselves with it before the really bleak weather begins.

A bird-table can be extremely simple in its form and construction, and is cheap to make, being simply a wooden platform either supported on a post or suspended from a tree. Ready-made bird-tables can also be bought from RSPB outlets or from garden centres. However, whatever the design of your bird-table, and whether homemade or purchased, there are several factors to remember when choosing its location.

First, the bird-table should not be in such a position that birds feeding from it are at risk from predators. It should be placed at a distance of at least nine feet

from trees and shrubs which could provide cover for cats and other predators. Cats and grey squirrels will readily pillage the food on the tables themselves if they can reach it – via, for instance, an overhanging branch. Some birds (dunnocks, for example) rely on gleaning the scraps which fall from the table on to the ground. There is also little point in locating the bird-

A cat-proof bird-table. Knitting needles driven into the platform deter feline predators.

Two methods of attaching the bird-table to its post

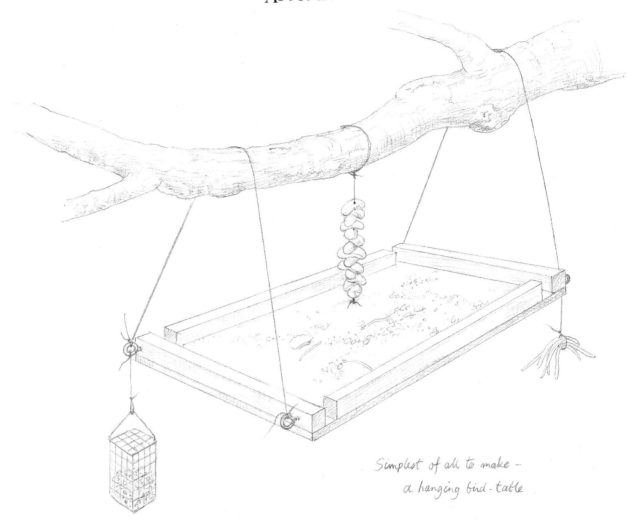

*Simplest of all to make –
a hanging bird-table*

table where you cannot easily watch the birds using it without disturbing them.

The materials required to make the platform are a piece of plywood, 12 × 18 inches and ½-inch thick (this must be of exterior, or marine, quality otherwise the wood will break up in rain or snow); a dozen brass screws or galvanized nails (care must be taken not to split the wood if using nails); a 52-inch length of 1 × 1 inch wood to form the coaming or raised rim around the edge of the table. This will stop food blowing off the table on windy days or being spilled by the birds. To construct the table, cut the 1-inch wood into two 12-inch and two 14-inch lengths and affix with screws or nails to the plywood. Leave a gap of about 1 inch at each corner to allow for drainage.

For the post-mounted bird-table you will need a 72-inch length of 2 × 2 inch wood; four 4-inch metal angle brackets; and a dozen ½-inch screws for fixing the platform to post. Screw the four angle-brackets to the table and post as shown. Treat all the wood with preservative. To position the table drive the post about 1 foot into the ground. A smooth metal post can be used instead, but a special adaptor will be required to fix the platform to the post. Cats will find a metal post more difficult to climb than a wooden one.

A hanging table is the other alternative. Birds are unconcerned by the free motion of a hanging bird-table so long as the table does not wave around too much in the wind. Sometimes it may be easier to affix the platform to an overhanging branch. To suspend the bird-table you will need four small brass or galvanized screw eyes which are screwed into the four corners of the platform. Use equal lengths of terylene or nylon cord (approximately 2 feet in length) to suspend. (Brass or galvanized chain can be used but this is more expensive.) Tie the cords to the branch to prevent the bird-table rotating in the wind.

A roofed bird-table has the advantage of keeping food dry. A sloping roof will also restrict the access of larger and more aggressive birds, such as starlings or sparrows which otherwise eat food left out for smaller birds. The roof is made by supporting a single piece of plywood on wooden supports. These are fixed to the corners of the bird-table so that it slopes down on one side.

WINTER

WINTER

In winter Britain's bird population is noticeably different from what it is at other times of year. The behaviour of the birds themselves is different too. The breeding birds of summer, certainly the insectivorous ones, have long since reached their tropical and sub-tropical wintering areas and have been replaced by others from further north and east. In summer most of them instinctively defend their own tiny patch of countryside or garden but in winter most birds forage in great communal flocks.

Whatever we may think, the winter climate in Britain is far more hospitable than it is in continental Europe or the Arctic, and provides open feeding most of the time for huge numbers of wildfowl, wading birds, thrushes and finches. None the less these are the hard times, the times that will test the resourcefulness of all birds, not least those born earlier in the year who have to face the unknown severity of winter for the the first time.

None of us who experienced the Great Winter of 1981–2 is ever likely to forget it. All other memories of hard winters began to pale into insignificance as the two most savage periods of frost and snow which any of us can remember gripped the country. Most birds can cope with extreme cold remarkably well provided they continue to find the necessary food to maintain body heat and keep themselves in condition: a heavy covering of snow produces worse problems for them than severe cold, but a combination of the two can be lethal in a very short time. Without access to food the birds will succumb to the cold through shortage of food rather than through inferior insulation.

The mid-December blizzard and freeze seemed to catch many birds unawares and there were few reports in the west of the country of the hard-weather exodus movements that often characterize severe spells in winter. The degree of cold was ultimate and deep and bird casualties occurred very quickly, many of the year's crop of young, inexperienced birds being amongst the first to fall. At home, on the third day of gripping cold, one rook lay feet up in the middle of the lane while another was found on the snow in the field nearby. Rooks are of course ground feeders, and these had been amongst those relying heavily on the sheep feeding-places nearby. The farmer had –

understandably – been getting agitated at the sight of forty or fifty hungry rooks sharing his expensive feed with the sheep and had prevented them from doing so the past week or so. Both rooks had died at night in the tree in which they roosted; by then both were already mere skeletons of skin and feather.

Within a few days the brook had frozen over in parts and only narrow channels of running water in mid-stream remained. Dippers are living proof of the fact that ample food conquers even the lowest temperatures. December is a month of noisy activity for dippers; undeterred by the cold, they constantly flew up and down the stream calling loudly. I watched the pair one morning from the bridge over the brook, where the branches of bankside hazel and rhododendrons were bent double with the weight of snow and locked into the ice of the stream; the cold froze the air in my nostrils and hurt the lungs when I inhaled but the dippers appeared not even to notice it. They bobbed mechanically on the edge of the ice and one after another repeatedly plunged into the freezing water, foraging under the ice and bouncing up again like corks. It seemed amazing that they could survive, but their life-giving harvest of hidden invertebrates was the key to the fact that they did so.

We fed many blackbirds, both on the bird-table and on the daily excursions up the lane, but the blackbird story I liked best from this period was the one concerning Mrs Eleanor Jones's Christmas tree. The good Mrs Jones bought her tree from the local greengrocer in Colwyn Bay where it had been stored in the back of a truck through the bitter days before Christmas. Mrs Jones erected the tree in her living-room and waited for the frozen fronds to regain their proper form. As they did so, after a few hours, a fine male blackbird which had evidently been frozen to his perch flopped out – apparently none the worse for wear!

At home we put out all the surplus apples on bare patches on the lawn and for three or four days a host of fieldfares joined the blackbirds and raiding jays that feasted on the apples right outside the windows. By the second freeze, in January, they had gone and at that time we did not see one; let us hope they had taken the hint and were further west, in Ireland, or south in France.

For those birds that won through the December spell to enjoy the relative bounty of a few New Year days of mildness, the second and – for us – even more

Dippers

bitter and damaging spell was the ultimate test. Many failed it. There were noticeable differences this time, too. Redwings and fieldfares escaped it by moving away and on the day when a thirty-six-hour snowfall started a friend of ours stood on the cliffs on the west coast of Anglesey and watched column after column of lapwings pour out over the cliffs and head for Ireland, together with hundreds of golden plover and skylarks. The wrens died this time, and so did the long-tailed tits, together with some other, less likely, birds. The red kites suffered and several of the precious stock were found dead or dying, for although there was carrion enough on the hills to feed a legion of kites it was either frozen rock-hard or buried under feet of snow, or both.

A buzzard fed one morning on the carcass of a cat killed on the main road on the edge of town; another picked off a hen pheasant, clean as a whistle, at a feeding station on a nearby estate, but the keeper bore it no enmity this time.

The strongest memory I retain from that winter is of the robins. They were ever-present and at our place it truly was the Winter of the Robin. They are normally fiercely territorial in winter but they managed a degree of truce, forced on each individual by the dire need to feed, but even so there was a constant series of posturing, 'ticking', bickering and sparring as their baser instincts broke the surface. Feeding the birds up the lane or lining the top rail of the bridge with grated suet and crumbs, we frequently had ten or twelve robins in view at once; they would call impatiently to everyone who walked out of the house and down the drive, and fly expectantly round our heads. In the autumn I had inadvertently scorched one of the fir trees by the brook when the wind caught the bonfire, and that side is still burnt and bare. My most lasting memory of the robins is standing near that tree watching nine of them sitting on the scorched branches, their red breasts facing me, looking for all the world like bright lights on a Christmas tree.

The Great Winter went as suddenly as it came and when the thaw set in, in mid-January, it thawed day and night thereafter. On the very first day of thaw those birds that were left forsook the bird-table and sought most of their own food; all that morning a green woodpecker yaffled in the wood as though in thankful celebration that he was one of the ones that had survived. A great spotted woodpecker called repeatedly too. Within days I had several telephone calls about blackcaps, normally summer visitors, which had survived against all expectations. Lapwings were on the thawing fields in no time at all (had they really flown back instantly from Ireland?). These are the ones that survived, the strongest and best, which will go on to breed in spring and set the recovery in train; none the less we shall count the losses for a year or two to come.

ROOSTING

Birds must rest and sleep at those times of day (or night) when they are not feeding: owls, therefore, will sleep by day and all our familiar garden birds by night. Wading birds and some wildfowl will roost either by day or by night because their life is bound to the daily cycle of the tides and much of their feeding is done by touch, for which reason they are not dependent on daylight.

Roosting, especially in winter, renders birds vulnerable. The selected roost site must fulfil two needs: namely, safety from predators at a time when the birds' normal responses are suppressed, and protection from the elements, especially cold. The need to maintain body temperature through the winter nights is paramount, and birds achieve this in several ways. First, and most important, they can fluff out their body feathers, thereby deepening the layer of warm air trapped within them. The amount by which such air is warmed may be only slight, but the survival margin in severe weather is often a narrow one. *In extremis* some species will cluster together, thereby

Long-tailed tits roosting together

Tree creeper roosting in a hollow in the bark of a Wellingtonia

reaping the benefits of a reduced total surface area and communal warmth. Long-tailed tits do this, and so do wrens – tier upon tier inside a nest-box sometimes! – and tree creepers, too.

Different species choose different places. Wildfowl find security from predators in the open water of a lake or on tidal flats, and can put up with the cold. Pheasants, terrestrial all through the day, roost in the branches of trees out of the reach of foxes. Grouse burrow under a cover of snow to take advantage of its insulating properties and quail (in summer) will roost in a circle on the ground, all facing outwards to maximize their communal vigilance.

It is an interesting exercise to try to find out where some of the regulars in the garden community tuck themselves away at night, for the subject of roosting has received little scrutiny and is poorly understood. The blackbirds and one or two chaffinches in our garden usually choose the depths of the evergreen rhododendrons or dense conifers, and one blue-tit disappears a foot or so along a horizontal scaffolding pipe each night (when he fluffs his feathers out he must fit it like a cork!). Wrens creep into the recesses of the woodshed or, where possible, will make good use of the past season's house martin nests.

Tree creepers have a special technique and are one of the species which actually roost vertically. Their favoured trees are wellingtonias and redwoods, the soft pliable barks of which are easily hollowed out to make little open-fronted roosting hollows. These little chambers are easy to recognize; there are often several on the same tree, and the one in current use can be identified by the streaks of whitewash below it. I used to wonder why they preferred to excavate their hollows so low down rather than going higher up for greater safety. Frequently they are only five or six feet up. But the bark gets harder the higher up you go, so I suppose that is the reason. What did tree creepers do before redwoods and wellingtonias were brought to

Cock pheasant roosting
in a tree

Starling

Britain a hundred and thirty years ago? Had a harder time, I suppose – literally. And how does such a feeble bird prepare this bedroom-scoop? Well, that must be the tree creeper's secret, but think about it. It is unlikely that anybody will be able to contradict your theory because I have yet to meet anyone who has seen a tree creeper at work.

STARLINGS

The European starling is probably the greatest avian success story of our time. It is hard to believe that only 150 years ago it was absent from most of Scotland, much of northern England, west Wales and the south-west peninsula. Since then starlings have recolonized their lost ground until, today, they have become almost ubiquitous throughout these islands. Moreover, with the help of emigrating Europeans over the past century the starling has an expanding global range already rivalled by no other land bird. The North American continent has been colonized from east to west and the pertinacious starling has footholds, unlikely to be relinquished, in South America, New Zealand, Australia, South Africa and India amongst other places. Only in South East Asia

Starlings

does it still have a major breakthrough to make.

The brash and forceful starling is few people's favourite, but it deserves our respect for its immense powers of adaptability and its success in exploiting a world changed so much by Man. Its bullying attitude on bird-tables and its unsavoury feeding places (rubbish dumps, sewage farms, and so on) do little to endear it to its human neighbours but its sharpest conflict with Man is caused by its mass roosting habits. It is less than a hundred years since the starlings were first recorded roosting on buildings in city centres, where their nightly presence in countless thousands is now known to all and disliked by most. Their droppings pollute and erode the ledges and stonework of buildings and foul the pavements below. All manner of deterrents have been employed, from wires and gelatinous paints to scaring devices and broadcast alarm calls, but the vast flocks remain.

In the country roosts of even greater numbers and density occur. There is one fifteen miles away from our home, near the English-Welsh border. If I drive along the main road an hour or so before dusk in winter parties of starlings will be crossing the road above the car for mile after mile, all heading directly for the sitka spruce plantation which is their vast communal roost. As the parties meet up en route from their daytime feeding they gather into vast surging masses. In their smaller parties they fly low, hard and direct, a thousand arrow-head shapes with one urgent purpose. As they gather into clouds and approach the roost they rise and fall, twist and turn like billowing, swirling smoke, their numbers uncountable and their sheer mass often darkening the evening sky. It is a memorable experience to be beside the plantation at this time. From every corner more arrive and the whole vast company wheels and swirls round and round in convoluted unison and by their thousands they drop steeply into the wood, leaving just as many still wheeling above and as many more still arriving. The din of their wings and the vibrating murmuration from the wood as they land in noisy chorus is deafening. Inside the plantation the ground is inches deep in nitrogen-rich droppings, more of which patter ceaselessly on to the ground. The centre of the plantation is a slum of dead trees, stinking slurry and broken branches, for many of the trees cannot support the sheer weight of starlings – shoulder by shoulder. The world's most successful bird has the same housing problem as its most successful mammal.

As night falls the invisible mass falls silent and sleeps until the morning sends the birds pouring out again to each corner of the countryside. If there are three hundred thousand of them here – and that must be a conservative guess – they will need some one and a half tons of leather-jackets, beetles, earthworms, waste food and so on before they return tomorrow afternoon; and they will need the same the next day and the next and the next . . .

Then in March and April the wood will empty bit by bit and the heaving hordes of starlings will wing their way back across Europe to the roofs and backstreets of Riga, Tallinn, Moscow, Leningrad and a thousand other towns to produce the next generation of eastern invaders.

WINTER FOOD

There is nothing more important for birds in winter than a constant supply of accessible food; winter will always be the time when the strong are divided from the weak – those that were born only to die in the first winter, through cold, starvation, predators or a combination of all three.

All the insect-eating birds, except for the most resourceful and hardy few, have fled for the south – flycatchers, chats, swallows, pipits and warblers – gambling the dangers of a journey of two thousand miles or more for the prospect of a bountiful supply of nutritious insects. The few faithful ones gamble the other way and stay with us in Britain.

It is a game of chance for all of them: should they face the hazards of migration or the equally dangerous risks of a northern winter? Each species must pay its money and take its choice.

Those insect-eating species which stay with us have their own carefully evolved formula for maximizing

the chance of surviving the winter. The stonechat is strongly western and south-western in its distribution and tends to keep to the coast in winter and so it normally benefits from the mildest of British weather, though some do migrate. Wrens are the ultimate explorers of cracks, crevices and clefts and these amazing little birds have one of the widest distributions of any British bird, both countrywide and altitudinally, and they prosper in towns, woodlands, farmland and remote islands and even mountains. Pied wagtails set up winter territories on riversides and similar watery places which they then defend vigorously against others of their kind. They rely on the constantly renewed supply of insects which the passing water brings with it and deposits at its edge.

One warbler only, the Dartford warbler, is truly resident in England; it relies on an insect harvest deep in the cover of gorse and tall heather. All these insectivorous birds are liable to suffer devastating losses in severe winters. Wrens, at times the most

Stonechats

numerous breeding species (probably more than ten million pairs in peak years), can be reduced to less than a tenth after winters like those of 1962–3 and 1981–2. The numbers of long-tailed tits, too, the only wholly insectivorous members of the titmouse family, are inevitably diminished in severe weather.

In recent decades greatly increased numbers of blackcaps, and to a lesser extent chiffchaffs, have been over-wintering in Britain. Chiffchaffs are entirely insect-eating, which makes them very vulnerable. Blackcaps, however, also eat fruit and berries and have learnt, in common with many other birds, the survival value of bird-tables.

The hierarchy at the bird-table can become a bit frustrating at times. The starlings dominate everything if they get the chance and several of our friends complained that they seemed to provide food for nothing else but half the starlings in Russia! (Millions of starlings from the East move to Britain and western Europe in winter.) Town pigeons can sometimes submerge everything else almost as effectively and house sparrows too can appear to dominate by sheer weight of numbers. But we have none of these on our bird-table at home – none indeed anywhere in our little valley! Our swinging bird-table has its own pecking order, with nuthatches taking priority over the great tits, blue-tits and coal-

tits in that descending order (though the nuthatches were conspicuously absent when blackbirds vied with each other for the right to feed). Marsh-tits popped in and out whenever the opportunity arose and a solitary surviving dunnock gleaned the spillings on the snow pile beneath.

Nowadays the number of households where food is regularly provided for birds through the winter is enormous and the effect of this on the survival-rate of garden birds has been very significant. Some people maintain elaborately provisioned tables, with food to suit all avian tastes, and replenish them as required; others toss scraps on to the window ledge whenever the thought occurs. There are one or two points to bear in mind when putting food out for the birds. Two are of fundamental importance: feed the right food, and, once you start feeding, do not leave off, because birds very quickly come to rely on you, especially when the weather is hard. They take most kitchen scraps gratefully and will avoid anything particularly unsuitable.

Bacon rinds, dripping, stale cheese, cake or biscuit crumbs, minced meat scraps and suet all carry high food value and will be welcomed. Scraps of bread – the traditional bird food – are actually at the poorer end of the spectrum; on its own bread, particularly the white, mass-produced, ready-sliced type, provides bulk but relatively little goodness. Cooked potato or stale cake is better, but all these foods are useful only to certain types of birds – sparrows, tits, nuthatches, robins, starlings and blackbirds amongst them. Peanuts, too, are a favourite food, either shelled or threaded on strings. Other families, notably the finches, need seeds; most forms of bird-seed mixes are popular, including the usual proprietary brands. Remember, however, that some species will only glean from below the bird-table; others will be reluctant to leave the open space of the lawn, while birds such as starlings will dominate the entire scene if they have a chance. Some of the more refined feeders and feeding baskets now available help a little with this problem, but you will probably never prevent the scourge of greedy and domineering birds.

Finally, it is only fair to make sure that any food or feeders provided are kept out of striking distance from the local cats and other predators. It is scarcely reasonable to lure the birds with much-needed food only to increase their chances of being snapped up in the process.

Dartford warbler

A blue-tit flies to join
the birds at the table.

The hungry crowd at the
bird-table comprises a nuthatch,
a great tit and two robins.

Most agile of bird-table
feeders, the blue-tit
loves shelled peanuts.

A coal tit pecks upside down at a coconut.

WINTER BIRDWATCHING

During winter birds are rather less in evidence throughout the countryside than they were in the warmer seasons. Many, of course, have migrated. Those that remain are no longer evenly distributed through the countryside: instead, they are largely concentrated in groups and flocks. The woodlands, for example, can be almost devoid of birds on some days at this time of year. This means that the birdwatcher must go out and find the birds in the areas in which they congregate in their winter flocks.

British estuaries in winter support vast numbers of wildfowl and waders from east and north Europe and for this reason river mouths provide some of the best and most exciting birdwatching. However, it is worth finding out about the timings of the tides before you visit an estuary to ensure that you go when the tide is rising and bringing the birds with it, otherwise many of them may be too far away to see. Inland waters, too, are much frequented by flocks of wildfowl, gulls and grebes, among others, and can provide good concentrated birdwatching; the same applies to many urban reservoirs.

Much of the focus in winter will be on watery places, but otherwise many people have favourite areas where they can regularly expect to find flocks of redwings and fieldfares, roaming parties of tits and their followers, or feeding throngs of winter finches, while optimists will hope to encounter a solitary great shrike, a group of colourful waxwings or other winter specialities.

Winter is also one of the times of year when sick or injured birds are most often found. At this season they are under pressure to find sufficient food and they are all the more likely to fall victim to cats, road accidents and similar misfortunes. Although it may be tempting to enjoy the opportunity of restoring a wild bird to health, remember that its long-term chances are already diminished and that only the fittest birds will survive.

Catch the bird and pick it up with great care. Carry it in a suitably-sized cardboard box or similar container. Handle the bird as little as possible. Sick and injured birds will usually keep still and quiet if placed in the dark. If you have to house them for a few days make suitable accommodation available: for example, a budgerigar cage, wire-fronted box or garden shed, depending on the size of the bird. Keep them warm (70°F, and higher for smaller birds). Cover the floor area with newspaper and change it daily to keep the bird clean. If a bird is sick, as opposed to injured, it is unlikely to survive long in

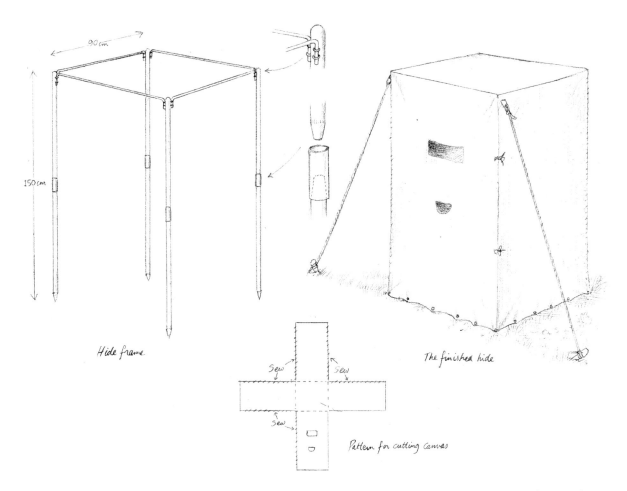

90 cm

150 cm

Hide frame

Sew   Sew

Sew

Pattern for cutting canvas

The finished hide

any case, especially if it was already weak enough to have allowed capture.

The most frequent injuries are fractured bones in wings and legs, flesh wounds, concussion and shock. After an initial examination, clean any wound carefully with mild disinfectant and put the bird to rest for a short while before providing food and water. If the bird will use a perch try to provide one.

Looking after injured or otherwise indisposed birds requires considerable time and effort, so it is not a responsibility to undertake lightly. Bear in mind particularly that no bird can possibly exist in the wild without wings that function perfectly; if you have a bird with a broken wing, or indeed other serious injuries, it is probably best to let it be humanely destroyed.

Lastly, never try to make a pet out of an injured bird.

It is very easy to frighten nesting birds to such an extent that they desert their eggs or their young, so intending bird photographers should act with extreme caution. A photographic hide is one way of approaching timid species without scaring them away, but ideally it should be set up a few days in advance, a little distance from the spot where you want to shoot, then moved slightly nearer until the required position is reached. Never cut away vegetation near a nest in order to take a better picture, for you will expose the birds to predators; also, strong direct sunlight could harm their young. Instead, tie back anything that interrupts the sight-lines just for the moment when you actually take the photograph. Do not photograph a nesting bird while it is in the process of laying its eggs: wait for a few days. Similarly, avoid photographing fledglings which are almost ready to leave the nest, for they may die if they try to do so too soon.

Proper canvas-covered hides can be bought from photographic suppliers, or, alternatively, you can buy interlocking metal poles to make a frame and make a cover for it (see pattern) out of any green or brown material you have to hand.

If travelling abroad, remember that in some countries a permit is needed for photographing nesting wild birds, especially if they are rare.

WHOOPER SWANS

Each year the whooper swans return faithfully to the fields near Penstrowed where the flood plain of the Severn is bordered by the soft wooded hills of Montgomery. Here they divide their winter between the good grazing in the valley fields and the open, windswept hills a few miles away where they roost and find meagre feeding round the fringes of three lakes there, Llyn Mawr, Llyn Du and Llyn Tarw (the Big lake, the Dark lake and the lake of the Bull). For company they share the dark, icy waters with a handful of goldeneye, tufted duck and teal and in the later part of the winter with a party of white-fronted geese.

They come from Iceland, these swans, from a summer home on scattered lakes in the lava plains and broad-bottomed glacial valleys of the great rivers of the interior. They bred poorly last summer and of the twenty-five birds here this winter only three are this year's young. I pass their fields every morning and often stop for a minute or two to watch them.

In most years they are two or three hundred yards from the road in a favoured field on the other side of the river, but this year they have taken a fancy to one very small field right by the roadside. They are haughtily unconcerned about the traffic which roars past all day, and I would never have believed that

these birds, which are normally so shy and which come to us from the wildness and isolation of central Iceland, would be so tolerant of people approaching them. On many occasions I and other passers-by have pulled into the gateway of the field and watched the birds from the open window of the car from as little as thirty yards away. Each time a car pulls up they slowly stop feeding and grudgingly move away with heavy gait, although without the awkward rolling step of the more familiar mute swans.

The families remain together even within the flock, grazing as a tight group, the gander alert and watchful. They are impressively large but at the same time aristocratic and elegant. All their movements are purposeful and deliberate, always unhurried and composed. They move forward, one occasional measured step after another, grazing casually with necks arching and extending; one looks up, shakes its head slowly, sits down infinitely slowly and grazes again from that position. The black feet and yellow and black bills are the only contrasts to the snow-white plumage. The bright yellow base to the bill extends in a wedge towards the tip and at close range the slight differences in pattern from one individual to another can be seen. In flight the wings produce an evocative rhythmic swishing, quite unlike the heavy throbbing of our resident mute swans.

During the two great freezes they disappeared

Whoopers fly with slow, powerful wingbeats.

A young bird on the water, with three adults.

Braking to land in a valley field.

Whoopers in a group on pasture.

completely, as they must do, for their feeding ground was wholly frozen and snow-covered, but each time, to my surprise, they were back on the first day of the thaw feeding hungrily on the open patches in the field. Where they had been in the meantime remains their own secret; nobody I asked had seen them anywhere else, nor had they turned up on the nearest coastline where the estuary is a sanctuary and a holding ground for many wildfowl.

GEESE

Out near the Shropshire border the riverside meadows lie wet and pools of standing water fill the hollows through much of the winter. These are goose fields, wet and splashy but perfect grazing for the geese. Each winter I go there several times, now out of habit as much as anything, for I remember with nostalgia the times in the 1960s and early 1970s when this was one of the great British wintering grounds for European whitefronts. These geese, wildest and most wary of all wild birds, move out from Arctic Russia as winter closes in and make for the western seaboard of Europe, breaking the journey into several easy stages, across the Gulf of Finland. A few thousand of them – numbers depending on the severity of the continental winter – cross to Britain. The bulk of these birds winter on the Wildfowl Trust grounds at Slimbridge in Gloucestershire, but the fields on the Welsh border were also important. As many as four thousand have whiffled down skein after skein to start grazing cautiously. They still come here but their number now is a dim shadow of what it used to be. This year as I scanned the fields I found a party of only 59 grazing on the frosted ground. Various reasons are put forward but still nobody really knows why they have left.

At the same time as this Severn flock reduced, the numbers started building up fifty miles south in the valley of the river Tywi, where there are similar low-lying meadows prone to flooding. In winter this is an exciting place not just for the geese but for other wildfowl, too; the best part is the area dominated by the stumpy ruin of Dryslwyn Castle on its impressive rocky mound in the middle of the valley. The castle mound dominates the valley, giving commanding views upstream and downstream. It is an ideal place for carrying out counts, or just for watching the birds. On a crystal-clear day at the end of January the fields

White-fronted geese and lapwings

around were dotted with birds. On the downstream side of the valley were golden plover and lapwing partly hidden in a fold in the ground near the river, some of the lapwing spilling over on to the muddy spit reaching out into one of the wide meanders of the river. Three herons were spaced out under the earthy bank on the far side of the channel, two alert and fishing, the third hunched and uninterested: presumably he had fed already. Many of the fields here are separated by straggling hawthorn hedges, and foraging parties of redwings and fieldfares were spread out in the fields from their refuges in the hedgerows. On the river two little grebes swam in the sunlight, diving in the slack water on the inside of the nearest bend, and a dozen mallard were dozing under the overhanging branches of the bankside willows. It was in these same fields the previous winter that I had watched well over a hundred ravens feasting on sheep carrion, after disastrous floods had swept down the valley. The ravens had been attracted like flies to the carcasses and gorged themselves to surfeit. When they were disturbed the flock rose, heavy and protesting, to fly around in a black, menacing crowd before slowly sinking down again to carry on their gruesome feast.

Upstream from the castle the geese held the centre of the stage, for some four hundred of them were feeding on a large, grassy field about six hundred yards away. The field was convoluted with the depressions of ancient ox-bows and former river channels; some of these flashes held floodwater and the geese were spread out amongst them, many in full view but others attenuated as they fed beyond the brow of the hollows. Some were just a series of heads, raised at intervals to check that all was still clear before sinking again to browse and thus disappearing from my view. Like the whooper swans, the geese have a secure family bond throughout the long migration and on the wintering grounds. Last summer's birds are distinct from the adults in having neither the smart white face patches nor the blotched black barring on the underparts of the adults. In the sunshine the orange legs and feet, continuously washed clean by the watery ground, are improbably bright. But last summer was not a good season for the geese in the Arctic, any more than it was for the whoopers, and there are many adults, partnered for life, without young this winter. On the wing they have a beautifully musical call, 'kow-yow', with a laughing

quality about it which can be heard as they climb out of the valley after dusk and head in long V's or skeins for roosting lakes in the hills or on the distant estuary.

All geese are constantly cautious and very wary of any approach. For this reason the areas they feed in must have a clear, all-round outlook; they cannot permit themselves to be hemmed in by hedgerows. This characteristic reflects the open flatness of the tundras of northern Russia or the glacial valleys of Spitzbergen, Iceland or Greenland. Of all the birds which visit these islands there is none which is more evocative of the wild northern swamps and tundras than the wild geese.

On the muddy flats of the North Sea coasts of eastern England the dark little brent geese arrive in mid-autumn from the farthest reaches of Siberia's Arctic shores. They are the most distant travellers of all our winter visitors and they feed on the trailing fronds of eel grass in the relative safety of the open, muddy, inter-tidal wildernesses.

Farther north and west the huge, flat salt marshes of the Ribble estuary and the Solway Firth support great flocks of pink-footed geese from Greenland and central Iceland, and the Solway has in addition large

White-fronted geese -
Long-distance travellers
from Siberia.

Greylag geese flying in a
V-shaped skein formation.

Greylag geese feeding warily in the flooded fields.

Dark-bellied Brents feeding
on eel grass on the tidal mud flats.

Pink-footed geese resting on the water,
while one keeps watch from the bank.

Barnacle geese
on the fields and tidal flats of Islay

numbers of barnacle geese. The stubble fields and mosses of lowland Scotland are a winter home to many thousands of pinkfeet and greylag geese.

The island of Islay off the west coast of Scotland is the ultimate Mecca for wild-goose chasers and with luck one can see as many as six or seven species within the course of one winter visit. It is barnacle geese for which Islay is most notable, however, and it supports around 20,000 birds which feed on the grassy fields through the day and at dusk retreat to the tidal flats on the two great arms of the sea which almost meet in the middle of the island. Here they drop down, skein after skein, for an hour or more to roost in their thousands on the shallow water or the tidal mud.

We know well enough nowadays that all the barnacle geese on Islay do indeed fly here across the north Atlantic from Greenland each winter. For a thousand years past, however, credence has been given to the far more interesting proposition that barnacle geese stem from the sea itself. The legend is that of the bird-fish, the barnacle goose being the living proof of the transmutation of fish-into-bird. Perpetuation of this belief also had a practical application, and there were people in western Ireland even in this century who considered it as perfectly

legitimate to shoot barnacle geese to eat on a Friday as they were 'more fish than fowl'.

The goose-barnacle (*Lepas anatifera*) is a marine crustacean which spends its life in the open sea and only occasionally ends up on shore. It sometimes turns up on western coasts of Europe after strong south-westerly winds, and it is this improbable progenitor which is credited with being the parent of the goose. Affixed to their own floats or attached to floating timbers by a strong stalk, these barnacles grow inside pale, brittle plates. The legend assures us that this is the fish-form of the bird hanging by its beak from the driftwood while developing its full feathered state within the shell, on completion of which it falls off and rises fully fledged from the water. Thus did barnacle geese originate each year, at least until they remained on *terra firma* and started to breed in Greenland!

CHRISTMAS BIRDS

The robin – as Christmas cards eternally remind us – and the wren have become an indispensable part of the legend of Christmas, although the origins and associations are often lost in the passage of time. We regard both birds with particular fondness as the season of goodwill arrives, yet their elevation to this position of goodwill is chequered, and by no means distinguished by the exercise of human kindness. Consider the poor unfortunate wren. The curious and ancient custom of the 'wren hunt', a singularly unfriendly and somewhat primitive activity, was widely practised until relatively recent years. It was specially associated with St Stephen's Day (26 December), and there were as many variations of the ritual as there were towns and villages in which it took place, from Co. Kerry to Suffolk and the Isle of Man. Essentially the miserable wren was hunted down and ritually killed, then it was borne ceremoniously through the town on an elaborate bier or 'wren

Robin

Nuthatch

house' by grotesquely dressed 'wren boys', to the accompaniment of pipes, flutes, drums or whistles, while the wren boys solicited halfpennies for the burial of the wren.

St Stephen is said to have been prevented from escaping his gaoler by a wren hopping on the guard's shoulder and waking him at the crucial moment (there are various other suggested origins of the wren hunt), a deed for which the tiny troglodyte seems to have paid dearly ever since.

In Wales they used to sing with delightful paradox as they carried the wretched bird around, 'Cussed is the man who kills a robin or a wren'!

The robin's original association with Christmas is more recent and revolves round the fact that Victorian postmen wore bright red frock-coats and were nicknamed 'robins', which is why the bird soon came to be portrayed on Christmas cards for delivery by the postmen. Legend reminds us – again there are many variants – that the robin obtained its red breast through scorching in Hell as he (or the wren he went to rescue) went to fetch fire for us here on Earth. Our thanks for its help seem to have been shortlived, for despite the perils which folklore warns us await those who kill a robin or a wren, we are also told of the virtues of the robin roasted on a spit. This activity is fraught with dangers, however, for if the spit is made of hazel the robin will begin to rotate unaided (don't try it for yourself, just take my word for it).

BIRDS IN THE LANE

As well as providing food on the bird-table and the tit baskets the family customarily feeds the birds (the same ones follow us all the way from the bird-table!) on the daily walks up the lane to exercise the dogs. The neighbourhood robins and marsh-tits wait impatiently each day and appear as if by magic in the deserted lane. The marsh-tits are particularly fearless, arriving the moment the first crumbs of cheese or suet are scattered; they feed around our feet and are soon joined by robins and one or two coal-tits. Blue-tits are less confiding and emerge only once we have moved on to the next spot; that is when the shy dunnock slips secretively out of the hedge bottom. A willow-tit comes now and again; the other day it was caught in nervous indecision having flown out for the food and then decided we were still a bit close for comfort. It stopped in mid-air and hovered perfectly, humming-bird-like, for several seconds before it thought better of it and left again. The nuthatches have their special spots on the lane and wait with a predictable certainty, like tollgate keepers charging their fee before we pass. They are both agile and surprisingly bold, and one of them has become adept at catching scraps on the wing. Two carrion crows have become rather a problem this year, however, appearing as soon as we are out of sight round the bend then rushing in for a quick mopping-up job.

GAME BIRDS

As the great snows began to melt at the end of the long winter I went up high on to the hills above home. The ground was still snow-covered and enormous drifts filled the gullies and engulfed the fences running over the hill. Even for a deep winter day high on the hills it was uncannily quiet. Neither the black, cronking form of a raven against an azure blue sky nor a single marauding crow carrying out its sepulchral tasks disturbed the scene; there was plenty of sheep carrion on the hills, but if it was not buried deep under the snow it was frozen hard as rock, so even the crows were on the lower ground around the farms.

The only birds I saw in two hours of walking were two red grouse which the dogs put up from remnants of a heathery patch of hill. Here they had survived the amazing cold grazing the dormant heather shoots under the snow, at night roosting deep in their own snow hole. They looked dark and vulnerable arcing across the hill against the whiteness of the snow, so unlike the ptarmigan on the high hills of Scotland which shed their mottled brown plumage for a pure white dress in winter – the only British bird to adopt a camouflage plumage for the winter conditions of the high mountain tops.

This weather is hard-going for the game birds on the low land too. Pheasants rely heavily on the food put down by the keepers in the woodland feeding areas. Otherwise the birds forage where they can for seeds, leaves, acorns and fallen berries on the woodland edges and on the uncovered areas of the fields; they often exploit the open ground around the sheep-feeding stations. At night they fly up to the branches of a dense fir wood. Even at this season the cocks are impressively gaudy, with their colours exaggerated by the monochrome of the winter countryside.

The native grey partridge is scarce in our part of the country; it is really more at home on the light soils and arable lands beyond the English border, and only once this winter have I seen a covey skimming over the roadside hedge and dipping down into a field of winter corn. The introduced red-legged partridge, a native of southern Europe, is more numerous as it has been released and successfully established on some of the hill farms for shooting purposes.

Red-legged partridges

Red grouse stand out starkly
against winter snow on the moors.

Partridge coveys remain together
through the winter.

The ptarmigan, bird of the highest hills,
adopts a winter camouflage.

Gaudy pheasants forage in the leaf litter.

GARDENS FOR THE BIRDS

To make your garden an especially attractive proposition for the bird community you need to provide water, food, shelter, shade and nest-sites. The water element could be a permanent feature, such as a pond, a bird bath or simply a dish of water on the bird-table. The rest can be provided by plants of different kinds.

The lawn itself is an important food-hunting area for birds. Trees are another priority, and the most valuable for birds tend to be native species because they harbour large numbers of insects on which the birds can feed. They are also easier to grow, in the main, than more exotic types. In autumn birds will feed on the fruit and seeds of many species of tree – for example, native yew, hawthorn and holly, hazel, oak, ash, cherry, willow and birch. Hawthorn, yew and holly can also provide convenient nesting places, and their berries will attract many types of bird, ranging from blackbirds, thrushes and starlings to the occasional waxwing in winter. Other useful berry-producing plants include rowan, or mountain-ash, and, among the shrubs, various types of cotoneaster and berberis (barberry) plants; the former include *Cotoneaster horizontalis*, *C. simonsii* and *C. integerrima* (which fruits late in the year), the latter *Berberis vulgaris*, the native plant, and, among the exotics, *B. darwinii*, *B. thunbergii* and *B. wilsonae*.

Blackberries are as much a favourite with the birds as they are with humans, so if you can spare a clump for them in a wild corner of the garden you will have a constant stream of avian visitors. Bullfinches tend to eat the blossom of fruit trees, especially when the ash crop fails, and all birds will enjoy eating windfalls from all kinds of fruit tree.

Among the climbers ivy, which has so many uses as garden camouflage, provides cover and nest-sites, especially for wrens and spotted flycatchers, and its flowers attract many different insects. Not only will it thrive in poor soil, but it is a prolific breeding ground for caterpillars; its berries, much enjoyed by woodpigeons, provide food in the bleak months of January, February and March. Honeysuckle also has berries (of particular interest to tits and warblers), as well as an abundance of flowers and a heady fragrance on summer evenings.

Stinging nettles, if you can tolerate them in the garden, are the food plant of several types of caterpillar – so necessary to the diet of nestlings.

Some birds eat the actual butterflies: spotted flycatchers are among the species which will be attracted by butterfly plants such as buddleia, hyssop and michaelmas daisy. Other flowering plants likely to encourage birds include teazle, cornflower, scabious, forget-me-not, cosmos, antirrhinum and sunflower.

Lastly, do not overlook the fact that some shrubs, such as rhododendron, privet and laurel, which may not be a food source for birds can none the less provide shelter and winter roosting places. Blackcaps often nest in rhododendrons, deep inside the bushes, and so, sometimes, do dunnocks and blackbirds.

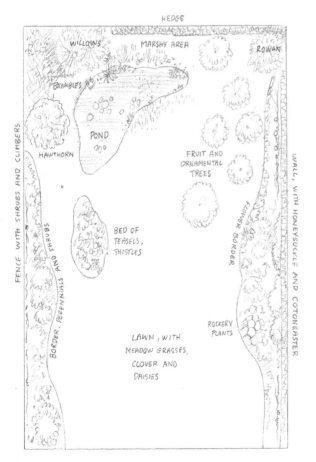

A garden plan

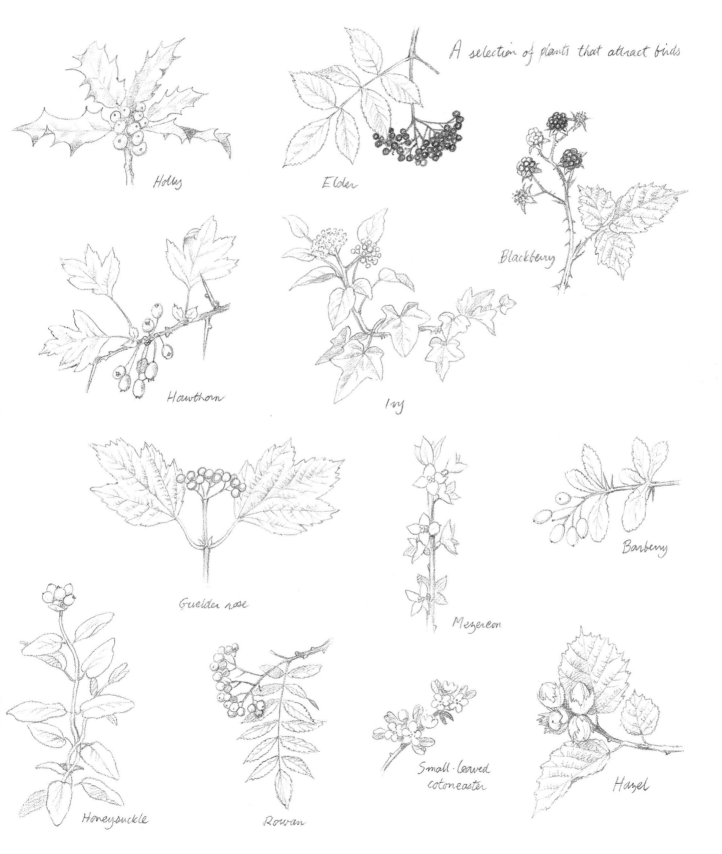

A selection of plants that attract birds

Holly

Elder

Blackberry

Hawthorn

Ivy

Guelder rose

Mezereon

Barberry

Honeysuckle

Rowan

Small-leaved cotoneaster

Hazel

BIRDS OF THE NORFOLK COAST

The winter wind cuts across the flat coast of Norfolk straight from Russia, uninterrupted by any hills this side of the Ural mountains, or so people say, and it can be uncompromisingly cold. Despite this, the mud flats, marshes, lagoons and sand bars all the way from the Wash to the low cliffs of Cromer are a hospitable paradise for innumerable birds of many species throughout the winter months. In summer and at times of spring and autumn passage, too, this coast is famed for its birds and its birdwatching and is one of the focal points in Britain for many thousands of birdwatchers through the year.

This year February produced several spells of warm, spring-like weather to atone for the bitterness of the earlier months of winter. I struck lucky when I visited this coast during one of these spells. In the first brilliant light of morning I walked alone out on the wildfowlers' track over the marshes at Thornham. As the track opened out on to the marsh a mixed party of finches rose from the ground in front of me and poured into the bushes alongside the track; greenfinches predominated, the bold yellow flashes on the wings and tails of the cock birds making a momentary splash of brightness against the browns and greys of the marsh. Solitary curlews rose from the muddy creeks on either side and flew, complaining, across the marsh.

The track, still alive with runnels of water from the receding tide, was sunk below the level of the marsh and the oozing mud made it slow-going. Ahead of me I could hear the disyllabic, conversational chuckling

Curlew

of pinkfeet geese returning from their fox-proof nocturnal roost out on the waters of the Wash, to feed now on the grasslands of the coastal marshes. A huge V-shaped skein of two hundred or so was flying low towards me and I watched motionless as they came closer and closer, passing directly overhead at no more than two hundred feet. Through the binoculars every detail was clear in the bright light until, at the last moment, the leader realized I was there, and with a violent twist the skein split in two and flew in opposite ways across the marsh.

On the edge of the sea beyond the marsh there were more geese, brents this time – small, dark-bellied birds with smoky black plumage and neat white 'necklaces'. All along this coast there were lines of them feeding on the open mud, in the shallow waters or sometimes grazing on the cultivated fields at the edge of the marsh. Redshank picked their way along the shoreline and a loose group of a dozen dumpy ringed plovers ran in short bursts over the wet mud where one of the marsh creeks fanned out across the foreshore. Even now in mid-winter there was a certain amount of posturing and flirting as the first tentative approaches to pairing were attempted and aggressive sallies were made between one cock bird and another.

At Holme-next-the-sea the spring-like weather was inducing flurries of activity from the shelduck pairs on the lagoon behind the outer line of dunes. Dunlin, redshank, curlew and knot were scattered amongst the spits and islands in the lagoon; gadwall – one of the loveliest of duck – and teal, already paired, were in full view, every detail of their plumage clear in the sunshine as they fed amongst the water-plants in the shallow pools. One or two snipe, motionless and part-hidden, skulked on the edge of the pool in front of us. Wigeon flew along the shoreline among gulls, lines of brent geese, and small parties of dunlin. We marvelled at the survival of a one-legged bar-tailed godwit, solitary but feeding well and seemingly in good condition. Just how does a shore bird like this come to lose almost all of one leg? Behind us a skylark gave voice to the promise of spring over the fields where several hundred pinkfeet fed. Out to sea we could see great crested grebes still in their quieter plumage of winter, rafts of scoter – the all-black sea duck from the north – and small parties of rangy and dishevelled red-breasted merganser.

Many other people were walking round the edge of this lagoon while we were there, but the birds showed

Snow buntings
from Scandinavia in varied plumage.

Gadwall - ducks of reedy broads and meres.

Teal - paired
as early as January.

Ringed plovers feed,
standing on the wet mud.

Parties of pintail spend much of the day resting and preening.

no signs of having been disturbed and for two hours or so a hundred or more people enjoyed some of the best birdwatching they could hope to find in Britain.

Further along the coast in a shallow, sandy depression behind the line of coastal dunes we found the snow buntings. They are numerous on this coast in winter, when they arrive from their summer home in the mountains of Scandinavia. None of our other regular winter visitors are more popular favourites than these colourful buntings. They rose as we crossed their area and circled widely in a twittering, undulating flock. They showered down towards the ground on the far side of the depression and just as it seemed they would touch down they wheeled away again; several more false landing attempts were made before they eventually settled amongst the seed-rich beds of sea-aster and samphire.

The individuals, predominantly mottled brown above and white below at this time of year, vary a good deal in colour. Some of the old males are almost in the bold black-and-white of summer and appear dazzlingly white on the wing, while many others look altogether browner when on the ground. On the wing the whole effect is of twinkling black and white and their alternative name – snowflake – is not only easy to appreciate but also evocatively appropriate.

A few miles further east Cley is as near to being the nucleus of this birdwatchers' heaven as one can get. More brent geese could be seen here, together with mallard, gadwall and shelduck, and in the sea of waving reeds the occasional 'ping ping' of bearded tits could be heard, but none was prepared to show itself at the tops of the tall reed-stems this time.

The pintail, slim and graceful with a long neck and fine bill, is one of our more elegant ducks. They breed sparingly in eastern England and Scotland and their

Snipe and mergansers

numbers are supplemented in winter by many birds from Russia. On one of the reedy pools at Cley, well provided with excellent viewing hides, two or three hundred pintail were gathered. Others flew in to join them as we watched: the flight silhouette of the drakes, with slender neck and pin-tailed rear end, is unmistakable. Pintail are partly night-feeders but a few of these birds were up-ending in the water, reaching deeper to the muddy bottom than any of the other dabbling ducks for the seeds, roots and tubers of water-plants. The rest sat around quietly on the water, some preening, others sleeping.

A touch of the exotic was added at Cley by a Chilean flamingo which towered, on one leg, pink and ludicrous, above scurrying parties of dunlin around its feet on Arnold's Marsh, its long neck coiled to allow its head to rest amongst the scapular feathers on its back. It looked as hopelessly out of place as indeed it was, an escape from someone's waterfowl collection.

Later in the day the RSPB reserve at Titchwell produced several hen harriers, hunting at low level over the reedbeds and rough marsh, and a short-eared owl to add to several others seen elsewhere during the day. The owl flew back and forth along the rough banks, perched for a while on a fence post and turned its head 180 degrees to stare at us, moon-faced, with huge lemon-yellow eyes. It flew again, flopping between the bushes on broad, rounded wings before passing out of sight beyond one of the sea walls.

NIGHT-OWL LISTENING

Even in the depths of winter there is plenty of activity at night. Life must go on and fox, polecat and owl must nightly search the woods and hedgerows for the steadily reducing winter supply of woodmice, voles, shrews and young rabbits. Many a still night in December or January is punctuated by the shrill barking of a fox, a chilling sound made more eerie by the intervening silences. In the early part of the winter the fox pairs are forming and the vixen is in season, but later on, when the bond is secured and mating is completed, the barking still continues as the two indulge in much noisy play.

It is at this improbable season that owls again become more vocal. Tawny owls are fairly noisy throughout the year. By mid-winter they are already

Tawny owl

intent on securing their breeding territories, for they can nest as early as mid-March. Their love-song – for such the hooting is – becomes regular as they set up their home base and seek to attract a mate. Both male and female 'sing', which is unusual in most bird species; but these are night creatures, so it is perhaps understandable that in their shadowy world sound must play as important a part as sight. One bird answers another; so on a still night you can hear the initiating effect one tawny often has on others in nearby woods. It is important that through voice recognition and stereotyped behaviour the female correctly recognizes the approaches of the male, for she has to reverse the solitariness and instinct to attack which have been the hallmark of her life since the last breeding season. He hoots, a long, quavering call of 'hoo hoooo', and she replies with a similar call. Sometimes the human ear can distinguish the individual differences: an owl always can. At other times she may answer 'ke-wick', and thus the eerie conversation continues through the night.

Even eerier than the tawny's lonely hoot is the doleful moaning of long-eared owls from small, wind-torn plantations on the hillsides, for this is another very early breeder. Its woeful sighing ('ooo-ooo, ooo-ooo') has amazing carrying powers and is audible on a quiet night up to half a mile away – to our ears, that is; no doubt the acute hearing of the owls can pick it up from one plantation to another at greater ranges than that.

The owl's night-time hooting serves the same dual purpose as the robin's or the blackbird's songs – to proclaim the tenancy of his territory and to attract the mate with whom he needs to share it.

CROSSBILLS

Different species can constantly confound us with their improbable timings and their healthy disregard of our conventional approach to seasons of the year. Now, towards the end of winter, the very earliest of breeders – the crossbill – is not only well under way with the build-up to its breeding season but may even have its young out of the nest (high up in the branches of tall conifers) and on the wing before we have accepted that winter is really on the way out. Crossbills can be remarkably early, sometimes laying as prematurely as December in Corsican and Scots pine plantations on the sandy soils in the southern counties of England.

These are birds inextricably bound to the cycle and supply of conifer seeds; they occur, therefore, in plantations of pine, spruce or fir and their unrepresentative breeding season is determined by the quantity of seeds which they extract as fast as possible from the cones in late winter and early spring to feed to their demanding young. They can remove the seeds at any time of year, but it is easiest when the cones are starting to open of their own accord. The crossbills' principal food trees have dropped their precious seed by springtime, and the crossbills are therefore committed to an earlier breeding season than any other British bird.

They are perfectly adapted to extract the seeds from the tough cones and their powerful crossed bills, with opposing and overlapping hooked tips, are ideally designed to nip out individual seeds from deep down between the scales. Heavy-headed in silhouette, they are adept at moving about in the swaying fronds of pines and spruces and, parrot-like, will make good use of their bills to haul themselves along the boughs. They happily hang upside down to feed: I have watched acrobatic and colourful feeding parties both in the tops of pine trees on the Norfolk heaths and in tall spruces in the big plantations on the Welsh hillsides, often betraying their presence with their hard, urgent 'chip-chip' calls. Many cones are twisted off by the feeding birds, which then grasp them firmly with one foot and attack the individual scales one by one to get at the seeds within. The scales patter down on the forest floor below and leave a characteristic litter of stripped stems and fragmented cones, which is sure evidence of the birds' presence.

The male crossbill is a splendid brick-red bird, although some individuals show variation and are paler pink or sometimes almost orange. At this time of year, as well as making frequent contact calls, the males sing a clear but somewhat unprepossessing jingle of notes, and if it is not the most captivating of songs, certainly the sight of the bright and bulky male singing from the topmost twigs of a tall spruce or larch on a bright winter's day is one of the finest sights the woodlands can provide for us at this time of year.

In another way, too, crossbills are interesting birds. Their main location is on the continent, in the great conifer belt of northern Europe, and as the cone crop varies widely from forest to forest year by year the crossbills move on each summer from one area of good harvest to the next, often many hundreds of miles away. Every few years, when continental numbers may be high and a widespread failure of the cone crop occurs, crossbills will 'irrupt' in enormous numbers and then appear widely and numerously in Britain where they are otherwise local and scattered most of the time. Many of the immigrants remain to breed in these new areas, but the numbers gradually diminish thereafter until supplemented again by the next summer irruption a few years later. The most reliable and numerous concentration of British crossbills is in the Highlands of Scotland, based on the remnants of the old Caledonian pine forests, where the birds – heavier-billed than those in southern Britain – are assigned to a separate race.

A male crossbill sings on a winter's day.

The crossed bill is a perfect adaptation for extracting pine seeds.

Crossbills are the earliest of breeders - a female sitting.

Young birds are out of the nest as early as March.

A crossbill feeds his young in their nest in a pine tree.

URBAN BIRDS IN WINTER

There is a widely-held fallacy that to see a variety of birds one must go into the countryside. Inner London is the most extensive urbanized area in Britain, yet over 160 different species have been recorded there this century and almost forty species have bred there in a fully wild state. Spring and summer may be thought of as the times when most birds are likely to be seen but in fact winter can be just as rewarding.

As the temperature falls city centres have the attraction of warmth, for the effect of tens of thousands of domestic heating systems, street lighting and the welter of human activity can raise the outside temperature a significant degree or two. City-dwellers do not need to be reminded that starlings, packed side by side on building ledges and fouling the pavement below, have been quick to take advantage of this fact. Other species, too, recognize the virtues of city life: pied wagtails, dainty waterside feeders relatively unconcerned about human proximity, feed around urban lakes, sewage farms and riversides during the day and sometimes roost in large numbers on building ledges or leafless trees in the light (and warmth) of streetlamps at night.

Food is the priority at this time of year. Urban areas provide ample scope for feeding in a variety of different forms, each of which will be exploited to the full in the hard months of winter.

Household waste produces almost an orgy of opportunity. Every day in the backyards behind the city streets starlings squabble and fight amongst themselves and vie with pigeons and house sparrows for the pickings and spillings from boxes of refuse and open dustbins. Throwing caution to the winds, they will disappear into the recesses of the bins, emerging like a swarm of angry bees when the alarm is raised.

Once the refuse has been moved to our insanitary refuse tips it becomes a vast free-for-all. Black-headed gulls (with only one small dark spot now left to remind us of the chocolate-brown head of summer), herring gulls and lesser black-backed gulls, jackdaws, crows and starlings produce a blizzard of activity all through the daylight hours, descending with relish on each newly arrived load. Thousands of gulls then resort to the convenient open reservoirs most of our urban areas also provide to wash, preen and roost at night.

The resident populations of thrushes, woodpigeons, tits, finches and others in town parks are supplemented by others moving in to share these fruitful areas for the winter. Beech trees, very

Black-headed gulls

Male black redstart

The wide realm of garden birds may now be swollen by the addition of a few shyer visitors. Siskins, small acrobatic finches, have learned to exploit peanut feeders; redpolls, also small and acrobatic, occur occasionally at seed tables, and at this season even sparrowhawks will not jib at the proximity of humans to take advantage of the host of potential prey.

Another bird to look out for in urban areas in winter is the black redstart, a very attractive foreign visitor which sometimes comes to Britain to breed, in spring and summer. Most migrate in autumn, but occasionally a few can be seen over-wintering in our larger towns and cities.

So let us not disdain the wealth of our urban bird life, for there is a great deal here to see all through the year. I can picture now a nuthatch on a winter's day working its way over moss-covered tiles on the roof of an old warehouse on the edge of a city park; it thrusts off the clumps of growing moss one by one to seek the woodlice and other invertebrates hiding beneath. Our cities are as much the homes of birds as they are of Man.

common in British parks, produce a large but unpredictable crop of mast each year and many resident species, including several of the tits, woodpigeon, chaffinch and nuthatch, depend heavily on beechmast during the winter. In years of heavy cropping the bramblings may well arrive too. They are northern cousins of the chaffinches and their winter movements over Europe are strongly determined by the annual changes in the strength of the beech crop. Brightly coloured birds in shades of orange, black and brown, they blend with their background as they forage on the ground among the fallen leaves.

At this time of year town parks can produce as much variety as suburban gardens to which the birds are lured by bird baths, feeders and bird-tables.

Male brambling

NESTING RAVENS

Flurries of snow are being driven across the moor, moving with them the tawny, deciduous fronds of molinia, the tussocky, unpalatable moor grass which clothes so much of the hills. An evil north-east wind cuts over the hills, swirling the snow and soughing through the creaking sitka spruce trees in the plantation which runs abruptly up to the other side of a deep and narrow ravine. The roots of the outer trees hook over the rocky edge, like talons gripping tight against the urgency of the wind. The cascading stream of water is caught by the eddies of wind and upturned in a fine spray. On this side of the defile two or three tough, skeletal mountain ewes, backs turned to the wind, rummage slowly amongst the tussocks for the finer grasses. They disappear as the snow swirls over them, and emerge again as it clears. This long winter has much sting left and the welcome call of cuckoo and evening drumming of snipe on the same hill are many weeks away.

On the crag on the other side of the narrow ravine, under the overhang of an angled slab of rock, is a great fortress of sticks; the base of it is five feet down from the rim, bedded into a cleft in the rock on foundations which, according to local knowledge, have held it there for six decades or more. The hen raven sits low on her nest warming the five blue-green eggs blotched with dark markings and bedded in the deep, wool-lined cup. Her back is flecked with snowflakes and the rim of the nest is white but she is used to winter in the hills and is oblivious to the cold. She looks up, cocking her head slightly as the resonant cronking of her mate rises up the defile. He beats up towards the nest, the wind at his tail, with deep and powerful wings. He is the Goliath amongst the crow family, thick-necked and with a huge pickaxe of a bill. At this time of year he scavenges the carcasses of those sheep that have failed to last the bitter, snowy winter and now provide him with an endless larder.

Ravens are birds of the open hill, camp-followers to the sheep industry in the uplands and more dependent on open-hill sheep walks for feeding than any other of our birds. Winter brings them rich pickings and is followed by a harvest of placentae and still-born lambs from the lambing flocks. This is the annual harvest they must cash in on for their young, and is the reason why they, too, like the crossbills before them, must lay their eggs in the depths of winter and rear their young with the flush of available food. They do it with an assurance and arrogance which befit their status, because nowhere in the world are ravens more successful or more numerous than in the hills of wild Wales.

Birds' seasons may seem strangely random until we appreciate the subtle reasons which determine their patterns. So while the ravens sit tight on their stick fortress, on the estuaries the wheeling winter flocks of dunlin, knot and godwit will remain intact for weeks yet before they fly north to their breeding grounds, for these will not be free of snow and ice for nesting until the raven brood is flying in noisy concourse high over the hills. On the rivers in the valleys dippers have been singing through the winter setting up their pairs and their territories, and any time now they will be building their mossy, football-sized nests under the bridge arches and on the weirs; the common sandpipers that will share the same riversides with them are still two thousand miles south in the warmth of the African sun, awaiting the urge that will bring them north to breed alongside the dippers, by that time well into their second brood. In our gardens and on the woodland edges tentative robins, great tits and song thrushes sing shyly and show the first faint signs of spring activity on warmer days; in the forest plantations the crossbills are already feeding their young. Over-wintering blackcaps, the hardy ones, still come to the bird-tables but their kith and kin – the mates many of them wait to find – still forage in thickets on the savannas and amongst the thorn scrub of tropical Africa.

Each bird has its own calendar; many species have a cycle which coincides with the broad seasons that we humans have identified, and we fit them into our accepted pattern, but many others show a refreshing disregard for such so-called normality. A calendar is for human convenience, but birds follow their own cycle, determine their own patterns and rely on powers of endurance, navigation, hunting, adaptability and physical manoeuvrability which are still outside what most of us can comprehend.

Ravens feed extensively on dead sheep, in the winter hills.

The hen raven sitting
on her nest,
flecked with snowflakes.
Her mate calls to her
from the ravine beyond.

BIRDWATCHER'S CODE

1. The welfare of birds must come first.

2. Habitat must be protected.

3. Keep disturbance to birds and their habitat to a minimum.

4. When you find a rare bird think carefully about whom you should tell.

5. Do not harass rare migrants.

6. Abide by the Bird Protection Acts at all times.

7. Respect the rights of landowners.

8. Respect the rights of other people in the countryside.

9. Make your records available to the local bird recorder.

10. Behave abroad as you would when birdwatching at home.

(Reproduced by permission of the Royal Society for the Protection of Birds)

USEFUL ADDRESSES

Selected Bird Reserves in the United Kingdom and Southern Ireland

Full details of the reserves listed, and many others, are available from the organizations concerned, on receipt of a stamped addressed envelope.

ENGLAND

Coastal

Farne Islands (National Trust), Northumberland*
Lindisfarne (Holy Island), (NNR†), Northumberland
Bempton Cliffs (RSPB), Humberside*
Titchwell (RSPB), Norfolk*
Cley Marshes (Norfolk Naturalists' Trust), Norfolk*
Blakeney Point (National Trust), Norfolk*
Minsmere (RSPB), Suffolk*
Havergate Island (RSPB), Suffolk
Dungeness (RSPB), Kent
Arne (RSPB), Dorset
Radipole Lake (RSPB) Weymouth, Dorset*
Slimbridge (Wildfowl Trust), Gloucestershire
Dee Estuary (RSPB et al), Cheshire/Clwyd*
St Bees Head (RSPB), Cumbria*

Inland

Fairburn Ings (RSPB), West Yorkshire*
Leighton Moss (RSPB), Lancashire*
Coombes Valley (RSPB), Derbyshire
Rostherne Mere NNR, Cheshire*
Ouse Washes (RSPB), Cambridgeshire
Rye House Marsh (RSPB), Hertfordshire
Nagshead, Forest of Dean (RSPB), Gloucestershire

SCOTLAND

Caerlaverock (NNR and Wildfowl Trust), Dumfries and Galloway*
Lochwinnoch (RSPB), Strathclyde
Vane Farm, Loch Leven (NNR and RSPB), Tayside
Fowlsheugh Cliffs (RSPB), Grampian*
Loch Garten (RSPB), Highlands*
Loch of Strathbeag (RSPB), Grampian*
Handa Island (RSPB), Highlands
Cairngorms (NNR), Grampian and Highlands*
Rhum (NNR), Highlands*

WALES

Whiteford (NNR), West Gamorgan*
Skomer Island (NNR and West Wales Naturalists' Trust), Dyfed*
Gwenffowd and Dinas (RSPB), Dyfed*
Tregaron Bog (NNR), Dyfed*
South Stack Cliffs, (RSPB), Anglesey*

NORTHERN IRELAND

Rathlin Island Cliffs (RSPB), Co. Antrim*
Castlecaldwell, Lough Erne (RSPB), Co. Fermanagh*

SOUTHERN IRELAND

Wexford Wildfowl Reserve (Irish Wildbird Conservancy), Wexford
Glen of Doons (Irish Forestry and Wildlife Service), Co. Wicklow
Derryclare (Irish Forestry and Wildlife Service), West Connemara*
Lough Graney, Co. Clare

† National Nature Reserves (NNR) are administered by the Nature Conservancy Council.

* An asterisk indicates that *some* parts of the reserve are normally open to the public without prior arrangement.

Principal European birdwatching organizations

AUSTRIA
Österreichischen Gesellschaft für Vögelkunde, c/o Naturhistorisches Museum, A-1014 Wien 1, Burgring 7, Postfach 417, Austria.

BELGIUM
La Ligue Belge pour la Protection des Oiseaux, Durentijdlei 8, 2130 Brasschaat, Belgium.

DENMARK
Dansk Ornithologisk Forening, Vesterbrogade 140, 1620 Copenhagen 5, Denmark.

FINLAND
Ornitologiska Föreningen i Finland, Zoological Museum, Prautatiekatu 13, SF-00100 Helsinki 10, Finland.

FRANCE
La Ligue Française pour la Protection des Oiseaux, La Corderie Royale, BP 263, F-17315, Rochefort, France.

GREECE
Hellenic Society for the Protection of Nature, Ornithological Section, Kydathineon 9, Athens 119, Greece.

REPUBLIC OF IRELAND
Irish Wildbird Conservancy, c/o Royal Irish Academy, 19 Dawson Street, Dublin 2, Eire.

ITALY
La Liga Italiana per la Protezione degli Uccelli, Lungarno Giuccairdini 9, Firenze, Italy.

THE NETHERLANDS
Nederlandse Vereniging tot Bescherming van Vogels, Dreibergseweg 166, Zeist 2740, Holland.

NORWAY
Norsk Ornitologisk Forening, Zoologisk Institutt, Norges Laererhøgskole, Rosenborg, 7000 Trondheim, Norway.

SPAIN
C.O.D.A., Aizgorri 5, Madrid 28, Spain.

SWEDEN
Sveriges Ornitologiska Forening, Runebergsgaten 8, 11429 Stockholm, Sweden.

SWITZERLAND
Verdand Schweizerischer Vogelschutzvereine, Secretary: Agnes Grünvogel, Gablerstrasse 36, 8002 Zurich, Switzerland.

UNITED KINGDOM
Royal Society for the Preservation of Birds, The Lodge, Sandy, Bedfordshire.
British Trust for Ornithology, Beech Grove, Station Road, Tring, Hertfordshire.
The Wildfowl Trust, Slimbridge, Gloucestershire.

WEST GERMANY
Deutscher Bund für Vogelschutz, Achalmstrasse 33a, D-7014 Kornwestheim, West Germany.

INDEX

Hutchinson & Co. (Publishers) Ltd
An imprint of the Hutchinson Publishing Group
17–21 Conway Street, London W1P 6JD

Hutchinson Group (Australia) Pty Ltd
30–32 Cremorne Street, Richmond South, Victoria 3121
PO Box 151, Broadway, New South Wales 2007

Hutchinson Group (NZ) Ltd
32–34 View Road, PO Box 40-086, Glenfield, Auckland 10

Hutchinson Group (SA) (Pty) Ltd
PO Box 337, Bergvlei 2012, South Africa

First published in 1982

Designed and produced for Hutchinson & Co. by
BELLEW & HIGTON
Bellew & Higton Publishers Ltd
17–21 Conway Street London W1P 6JD

Typeset by Tradespools Ltd
Colour separations by Fotographics Ltd
Printed and bound in Great Britain by Hazell Watson and Viney Ltd

ISBN 0 09 149490 7